JOSH MOSEY

# MAN OF PURPOSE

## 100 DEVOTIONS FOR THE ASPIRING LIFE

BARBOUR
PUBLISHING

Published by Barbour Publishing, Inc., 1810 Barbour Drive, Uhrichsville, Ohio 44683, www.barbourbooks.com

*Our mission is to inspire the world with the life-changing message of the Bible.*

Member of the
Evangelical Christian
Publishers Association

Printed in China.

### *Men, the world needs you.*
### *Celebrate true masculinity with this book.*

Masculinity has come under fire in recent years, but the world needs Christian men like never before. *Man of Purpose: 100 Devotions for the Aspiring Life* celebrates manhood, the kind that honors God, loves and supports others, and makes a positive difference in our world.

Each reading centers on a needful biblical character quality, encouraging you to "be the man"—the man who

- helps the needy
- prays without ceasing
- respects women
- gives cheerfully
- anticipates Jesus' return

You'll be challenged and encouraged to fill your God-given role in your home, your workplace, your community, and your world.

# BE THE MAN WHO
# LIVES INTENTIONALLY

*Good planning and hard work lead to prosperity,*
*but hasty shortcuts lead to poverty.*
PROVERBS 21:5 NLT

As a rule, people don't drift toward success. If life is a river, success is always upstream. We won't get there by floating along. We have to go against the flow. The first step to becoming a man of purpose is knowing what success looks like. Only when we have a destination can we be intentional about getting there.

The world measures success in terms of money, personal accomplishments, and possessions. It measures worth by the number of friends we have on social media and how we look physically. Worldly success compares people to other people. Achieving by the world's standards does require good planning and hard work—but when our lives are over, this world's adoration will be meaningless as we stand before God.

Don't waste time comparing yourself to other people. To see if we are moving toward success, we must compare ourselves to our Creator. Do we value what God values? Do we love as God loves? Do we forgive like God forgives? When people look at us, do they see God clearly?

As with worldly achievements, true biblical success also requires a plan and hard work. Not only will we go against the flow of the world's definition of success, we'll have to fight our own inclinations toward laziness, selfishness, and pride.

Living intentionally means wading upstream, step by step, motivated by God's love within us. It means making time to read God's Word and pray. Then we can move forward with confidence, avoiding the pull of the river's flow on our feet.

There are no shortcuts to becoming a man of purpose. . .only the next step in the right direction.

---

*How intentional are you in Bible reading and prayer? Are there areas in which you are drifting instead of moving upstream?*

# BE THE MAN WHO
# HELPS THE NEEDY

*Whoever is kind to the poor lends to the LORD,
and he will reward them for what they have done.*
PROVERBS 19:17 NIV

The saying "Give a man a fish and he'll eat for a day, but teach a man to fish and he'll eat for a lifetime" isn't from the Bible. Though its exact source is unclear, a similar statement was used in an 1885 novel by Anne Ritchie, the daughter of novelist William Makepeace Thackeray. This saying is meant to inspire us toward fixing societal problems, but it's sometimes used to justify inaction.

When we see someone who's hungry, we might say, "I don't have time to teach them how to fish." If we see someone who's cold, we might respond, "I don't want to give them a handout and make them feel worse."

In Matthew 25, Jesus told His disciples a story about a king who called together two groups of people. The first group took care of those in need and the king praised them as though they had met his own needs. When this group asked when they met the king's needs, he responded, "Truly I tell you, whatever you did for one of the least of these brothers and sisters of mine, you did for me" (Matthew 25:40 NIV).

The second group—who did nothing for those in need—was rebuked and sent away to eternal punishment. Why? Matthew 25:45 (NIV) says, "Truly I tell you, whatever you did not do for one of the least of these, you did not do for me."

We don't have to choose between giving people a fish and teaching them how to fish. We should do both. We aren't only serving the person in need anyway. We're showing love to the King of Kings.

---

*How can you take care of another person's immediate needs today? How can you change the larger problem that caused their needs?*

# BE THE MAN WHO WEARS GOD'S ARMOR

*Therefore, put on every piece of God's armor so you will be able to resist the enemy in the time of evil. Then after the battle you will still be standing firm.*
EPHESIANS 6:13 NLT

---

There is an unseen battle raging all around us. It affects the choices we make, the way we see the world, and how we treat others. Ephesians 6:12 (NLT) says, "For we are not fighting against flesh-and-blood enemies, but against evil rulers and authorities of the unseen world, against mighty powers in this dark world, and against evil spirits in the heavenly places."

How do we defend ourselves against "mighty powers" we cannot see? With spiritual armor the world doesn't recognize.

Ephesians 6:14–17 (NLT) says, "Stand your ground, putting on the belt of truth and the body armor of God's righteousness. For shoes, put on the peace that comes from the Good News so that you will be fully prepared. In addition to all of these, hold up the shield of faith to stop the fiery arrows of the devil. Put on salvation as your helmet, and take the sword of the Spirit, which is the word of God."

Truth and righteousness are not abstract concepts when it comes to our protective belt and body armor. To protect ourselves from the devil's schemes, we must know that Jesus' sacrifice was sufficient for our sins and that God has given us His righteousness as a gift. With this truth comes peace, since nothing can separate us from God's love. Our faith in God and in His love keeps the devil's lies from doing us harm. Our helmet of salvation is designed to keep these truths in our mind. When we do encounter doubts, we have the Word of God to guide us back to the truth.

God's armor is built on truth. Becoming a man of purpose means digging into the truth of His Word daily. The more we do, the more we'll recognize Jesus' sacrifice, which gave us God's righteousness, which leads to peace in His love for us.

---

*How confident are you in your salvation?*
*Why is truth the key to defending ourselves*
*against the enemy's schemes?*

# BE THE MAN WHO WIELDS HIS SWORD

*For the word of God is alive and active. Sharper than any double-edged sword, it penetrates even to dividing soul and spirit, joints and marrow; it judges the thoughts and attitudes of the heart.*

HEBREWS 4:12 NIV

---

Making a sword isn't terribly complicated. Blacksmiths start with a chunk of raw iron. The iron must be heated so impurities bond and float to the surface for easy removal. Iron that is free of impurities, called steel, is easier to shape, being both strong and flexible.

The brick of steel is slowly drawn out by repeatedly being heated and beaten into the shape of the sword. The sword is then heated again and rapidly cooled in oil for additional strength. Once strong enough, it is heated again and the point and edges are thinned and sharpened.

The Roman gladius was a double-edged sword used in Jesus' day. Although single-edged swords were better for swinging, double-edged swords were better for stabbing. And, having two edges, the weapon was dangerous for an enemy to grab at.

Hebrews 4:12 compares the Word of God to just such a sword. Scripture is free from impurities and has been shaped into something both strong and flexible. It is double-edged, intended to pierce hearts, not glance off armor. And when our enemies try to take God's Word away from us, they cannot help but be affected by it as well.

Our sword is not only a defensive weapon against the world. It is most useful when used on ourselves. By allowing the Word of God to pierce our own hearts, to judge our thoughts and attitudes, we become like the sword itself: free from impurities and shaped into something useful by the hands of the master blacksmith.

Our shaping (the heating and hammering of life's difficulties) will never be comfortable, and our sharpening (spending time in God's Word and prayer) will always take time. But being a man of purpose requires both.

---

*What impurities do you need to allow God to remove from your life? How are you being shaped to better serve God's purposes?*

# BE THE MAN WHO RESPECTS WOMEN

*And he began to speak boldly in the synagogue:
whom when Aquila and Priscilla had heard,
they took him unto them, and expounded unto
him the way of God more perfectly.*
ACTS 18:26 KJV

Apollos was a smart guy. According to Acts 18:24 (KJV), he was "an eloquent man, and mighty in the scriptures." But he still didn't have the full picture.

Apollos believed in the teachings of Jesus and strongly declared what he knew, but it wasn't until he arrived in Ephesus and encountered a married couple—Aquila and Priscilla—that he finally came to a full knowledge of Christ's sacrifice and resurrection.

In 1 Corinthians 3:5–6 (NIV) Paul recognizes Apollos as a fellow missionary when he says, "What, after all, is Apollos? And what is Paul? Only servants, through whom you came to believe—as the Lord has assigned to each his task. I planted the seed, Apollos watered it, but God has been making it grow."

But what would have happened if Apollos hadn't listened to both Aquila *and* Priscilla? The Bible mentions them both, which is interesting because it could have easily left Priscilla out. After all, in ancient times, women stood on the lowest rung of the social ladder. Their testimonies were inadmissible in Jewish courts.

If Apollos had similarly ignored Priscilla's contribution, the message of the Gospel would have been hindered. Because he listened, however, he convinced many people that Jesus was the Messiah the Jews had been waiting for (see Acts 18:27–28).

Although women have gained a lot of ground culturally since Bible times, some men still see them as less than equal. They are treated with less respect, viewed as weaker people, and allowed fewer opportunities to be heard.

Becoming a man of purpose, as Apollos was, means rejecting society's views toward women and respecting them as equal bearers of God's image. It means listening to them, as Apollos did, and giving them opportunities to speak, as Aquila did.

---

*How could you better listen to the women in your life? How could you create more opportunities for women to be heard?*

# BE THE MAN WHO KEEPS ON PRAYING

*And pray in the Spirit on all occasions
with all kinds of prayers and requests.
With this in mind, be alert and always
keep on praying for all the Lord's people.*
EPHESIANS 6:18 NIV

---

If the armor of God is our defense in spiritual battles and the Word of God is our weapon, prayer is our plan of attack.

Many men use prayer as little more than a mealtime ritual, as a last resort in times of crisis, or as a spiritual shopping cart, asking God to cover the payment. In reality, prayer is the most active thing you can do to strengthen your relationship with God.

After listing each piece of God's armor, the apostle Paul writes in Ephesians 6:18 (NIV), "And pray in the Spirit on all occasions with all kinds of prayers and requests. With this in mind, be alert and always keep on praying for all the Lord's people."

Paul didn't leave much ambiguity with how we

should pray. On which occasions? On all occasions. How? With all kinds of prayers and requests. For whom? For all the Lord's people. How often? Always.

A man of purpose actively prays. We should certainly thank God for our meals, pray for help in times of crisis, and even go to God with the things we want (as long as what we want is what He wants for us). But our prayer life should never stop there.

We should also pray for forgiveness when we sin. We should lift up the requests of other Christians in prayer. We should pray for God to have His way in our hearts, our families, our work, our future, and our nation. We should praise God for who He is and what He has done.

Don't know how to start? Pray about it!

---

*What aspect of prayer might be missing from your prayer life? Is there anything you don't feel like praying about? (Hint: This is probably the most important thing to pray about.)*

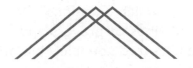

# BE THE MAN WHO GIVES CHEERFULLY

*You must each decide in your heart how much to give. And don't give reluctantly or in response to pressure. "For God loves a person who gives cheerfully."*
2 CORINTHIANS 9:7 NLT

Seeds are incredible. When planted in good soil and nourished by sunlight and water, seeds become plants, which, in turn, make more seeds, enabling one small seed to grow exponentially in number within a short time.

In his second letter to the church at Corinth, Paul uses this agrarian example to illustrate generosity. Second Corinthians 9:6–8 (NLT) says, "Remember this—a farmer who plants only a few seeds will get a small crop. But the one who plants generously will get a generous crop. You must each decide in your heart how much to give. And don't give reluctantly or in response to pressure. 'For God loves a person who gives cheerfully.' And God will generously provide all you need. Then you will always have everything you need and plenty left over to share with others."

God has blessed us with resources to grow His kingdom. Whenever we plant generously with the resources He's given, our increase will be exponential.

What does this have to do with giving *cheerfully*? Planting seeds isn't a fun process. It's hard work! But a farmer can be cheerful because he knows his seeds will become a harvest. And just like with actual plants, the harvest is God's responsibility, not ours.

While generosity is often associated with finances, God has given us resources that have nothing to do with our bank account. We can be generous with our time, our attention, and our help. We can loan our tools and share our food. We can even be generous with our compliments.

Whenever we give cheerfully to others, God will ensure we have enough to keep giving.

---

*What resources could you give cheerfully to others? How have others given cheerfully to you?*

# BE THE MAN WHO ANTICIPATES JESUS' RETURN

*"It will be good for those servants whose master finds them watching when he comes. Truly I tell you, he will dress himself to serve, will have them recline at the table and will come and wait on them."*
LUKE 12:37 NIV

Jesus told us to keep watch for His return. That alone should be enough of a reason to do so, since Jesus is God and we should listen and act on whatever He says. But Jesus didn't just give us a command. He also told us a story to show what kind of God He is.

Jesus says in Luke 12:35–38 (NIV), "Be dressed ready for service and keep your lamps burning, like servants waiting for their master to return from a wedding banquet, so that when he comes and knocks they can immediately open the door for him. It will be good for those servants whose master finds them watching when he comes. Truly I tell you, he will dress himself to serve, will have them recline at the table and will come and wait on them. It will be good for those servants whose master finds them ready, even if he comes in the middle of the night or toward daybreak."

The servants' job was to be ready whenever their master returned. They didn't need any additional incentive. But the master did reward the prepared servants by trading places with them at his arrival.

Becoming a man of purpose means keeping watch for Jesus' return, not just because He told us to, but because we also know He rewards obedience. We need to be dressed and ready with our lamps burning bright, no matter how late we think it might be.

How are we to dress? Revelation 19:8 (NIV) describes our garments as "righteous acts of God's holy people." And how can we keep our lamps bright? Matthew 5:16 (NIV) says, "In the same way, let your light shine before others, that they may see your good deeds and glorify your Father in heaven."

---

*What righteous acts can you do to make sure you're dressed? What good deeds can you do to shine God's light?*

# BE THE MAN WHO
# SPENDS TIME WISELY

*So be careful how you live. Don't live like fools,
but like those who are wise. Make the most
of every opportunity in these evil days.*
Ephesians 5:15–16 nlt

---

As we eagerly anticipate Jesus' return by living righteously, we need to be especially aware of how we spend our time.

Have you ever felt like time has sped up since you were young? Our whole lives were ahead of us then, and every experience was new. As we get older and have fewer new experiences, our lives become stuck in a routine while whole days pass in what feels like seconds.

In 2011, journalist Matt Danzico documented his personal effort to slow his perception of time—an experiment he called "The Time Hack." Danzico was inspired by research that suggested new experiences could alter a person's perception of time, so for one year, he attempted to do something new every day.

By using a stopwatch to accurately time each experience, then noting how much time he felt had passed, Danzico was able to measure how much experiential time he gained or lost.

He experienced the greatest percentage of time gain on Day 114 when he performed a burial service for a deceased houseplant (perceived time: 33 minutes 21 seconds; actual time: 11 minutes 9 seconds) and lost the greatest percentage of time on Day 26 when he hosted a toilet paper unraveling competition (perceived time: 32 seconds; actual time: 7 minutes 23 seconds). Over the year, Danzico experienced an extra 14 hours, 43 minutes and 29 seconds.

While Danzico's activities were mostly trivial, he was proactive about his time use. Whenever you find time slipping away, do something new. Memorize a whole book of the Bible. Talk to a stranger about Jesus. Pray for someone you've never prayed for. Not only will your experience of time slow down, but you'll be spending your time on things that matter.

---

*What is something spiritual you've never done before? When can you do it within the next week?*

# BE THE MAN WHO
# SAYS WHAT HE MEANS

*"All you need to say is simply 'Yes' or 'No';
anything beyond this comes from the evil one."*
MATTHEW 5:37 NIV

---

In the United States, incoming presidents often take the oath of office by placing their left hand on a Bible while swearing to uphold the Constitution. George Washington began the practice on April 30, 1789, and presidents have continued it into modern times.

According to *The New Yorker* contributor Hannah Rosefield, the use of oath books in a legal setting dates back to ninth-century England, when certain transactions were conducted at the altar with participants swearing on a Gospel book. A few centuries later, English courts adopted the practice. Rosefield writes, "By placing a hand on the book and then kissing it, the oath-taker is acknowledging that, should he lie under oath, neither the words in the Bible nor his good deeds nor his prayers will bring him any earthly or spiritual profit. In time, this became standard legal procedure—all witnesses swearing to tell the truth, the whole truth, and nothing but the truth—and made its way into American courts. British witnesses today still take their oaths 'by Almighty God,' as American oath-takers conclude theirs with 'so help me God.' "

We might be tempted to affirm the practice of swearing our truthfulness by the Bible or by invoking God's name, but doing so isn't biblical.

In Matthew 5:33–37, Jesus prohibits taking oaths. He wants His followers to have such integrity that their truthfulness is never called into question. A true man of purpose says what he means and keeps his word. When his integrity is intact, his words will be believable.

Next time you feel tempted to swear something is true, remember how trustworthy most politicians are and ask yourself if the oath will boost your credibility.

---

*Do you ever say things like, "No really, I'm telling the truth!"? What are some better ways to convince people?*

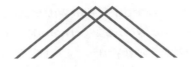

# BE THE MAN WHO RUNS FOR THE PRIZE

*Don't you realize that in a race everyone runs,*
*but only one person gets the prize? So run to win!*
1 CORINTHIANS 9:24 NLT

At the time of Paul's missionary journeys, the city of Corinth hosted the biennial Isthmian Games, second only to the Olympic Games in popularity. The Isthmian Games were an ancient festival of athletic and musical competitions held in honor of the Greek god Poseidon. The victors of each competition were crowned with a pine wreath.

In his letter to the church at Corinth, Paul borrowed the imagery of the Isthmian Games to teach a spiritual truth. First Corinthians 9:24–27 (NLT) says, "Don't you realize that in a race everyone runs, but only one person gets the prize? So run to win! All athletes are disciplined in their training. They do it to win a prize that will fade away, but we do it for an eternal prize. So I run with purpose in every step. I am not just shadowboxing. I discipline my body like an athlete, training it to do what it should. Otherwise, I fear that after preaching to others I myself might be disqualified."

The man of purpose runs with "purpose in every step." Intentional in action and consistent in attitude, he keeps his eyes on the eternal prize.

Philippians 3:13–14 (NLT) says, "No, dear brothers and sisters, I have not achieved it, but I focus on this one thing: Forgetting the past and looking forward to what lies ahead, I press on to reach the end of the race and receive the heavenly prize for which God, through Christ Jesus, is calling us."

Successful athletes discipline themselves, giving up junk food and regularly training for their sport. Successful Christians discipline themselves too. Refusing to dwell on past sins, they run forward in grace, committing their steps to God's glory.

---

*Are you looking backward or forward as you run? What practices might you need to drop in order to run more freely?*

# BE THE MAN WHO DENIES HIMSELF

*Then said Jesus unto his disciples, If any man
will come after me, let him deny himself,
and take up his cross, and follow me.*
MATTHEW 16:24 KJV

Death by crucifixion wasn't fun. In fact, the word *excruciating* was invented just to describe how painful it was. If it had been pleasant, Jesus wouldn't have asked for another way.

Mark 14:36 (NIV) records His prayer in the garden of Gethsemane on the night of Judas's betrayal: " 'Abba, Father,' he said, 'everything is possible for you. Take this cup from me. Yet not what I will, but what you will.' "

Jesus submitted His future to God, understanding the grave necessity of the cross yet still refusing to run. He lived out the command He gave to His disciples in Matthew 16:24 by denying Himself and taking up His cross to pay for the world's sin.

Life isn't always fun. There will always be jobs we'd

rather not do. If washing dishes or folding clothes isn't your cup of tea, it's still better than the cup Jesus drank when He died for our sins. When we deny our wants in order to serve others, we take up our cross. When we give up our rights for someone's convenience, we take up our cross. When we lift others up instead of stealing the spotlight, we take up our cross.

Men of purpose find ways to serve others sacrificially, stepping outside their comfort zones to pass on God's undeserved love. Is it fun? No. Is it excruciating? Sometimes. The greater the pain, however, the better we will understand what Jesus endured for us.

---

*What potentially helpful job do you dislike the most? How can you deny yourself to better understand Jesus today?*

# BE THE MAN WHO ENCOURAGES OTHERS

*So encourage each other and build each
other up, just as you are already doing.*
1 THESSALONIANS 5:11 NLT

---

When tragedy strikes—whether natural disaster, death, or destruction of property—grief is a natural response. However, while grief has its place, not everyone knows how to move past it.

A man of purpose always shares hope in tragedy. He encourages the grief-stricken by empathizing with their pain, meeting their needs, and showing them—by example—his eternal perspective.

When tragedy struck the church of Thessalonica, they didn't know how to grieve, so Paul wrote, "And now, dear brothers and sisters, we want you to know what will happen to the believers who have died so you will not grieve like people who have no hope" (1 Thessalonians 4:13 NLT).

Our hope is in Jesus and the enduring salvation He gives.

God can—and does—cause good to spring from bad situations, but before we quote Romans 8:28 to the grieving ("And we know that God causes everything to work together for the good of those who love God and are called according to his purpose for them," NLT), we must quote Romans 12:15–16 to ourselves "Be happy with those who are happy, and *weep with those who weep*. Live in harmony with each other. Don't be too proud to enjoy the company of ordinary people. And don't think you know it all!" (NLT, emphasis added).

We won't always know what to say or how to build others up, but our quiet presence should communicate God's love. The greatest needs of our community are met whenever we show people our hope of a glorious future beyond all grief. Encouragement starts with listening and ends with sharing our hope.

---

*How has someone shared hope with you before? What are some practical ways to meet someone's need in times of loss?*

# BE THE MAN WHO
# TESTS FALSE TEACHING

*Dear friends, do not believe every spirit, but test the spirits to see whether they are from God, because many false prophets have gone out into the world.*
1 JOHN 4:1 NIV

---

According to researchers at Princeton University and New York University's Social Media and Political Participation Lab, Americans over the age of sixty-five were much more likely than younger citizens to spread "fake news" on Facebook during the 2016 presidential election.

On the other hand, a study by *Forbes* found millennials are six times more likely to give out credit card information over the phone than Gen X or Baby Boomers.

While media and financial literacy—the ability to recognize fake news or scams—are vital to our well-being, spiritual discernment is even more important to Christians of all ages. False doctrine doesn't only affect our earthly conduct; it can bring eternal consequences. Fortunately, as with nonspiritual matters, we can check what we hear against the truth.

First John 4:1 encourages believers to have a healthy skepticism toward spiritual matters lest false prophets undermine our faith. Just as we discern the truth of political information on social media, we should apply our minds even more carefully when matters of salvation are discussed. By knowing God's Word by heart, we can separate the truth from a false prophet's lies.

While some Christian teachings do sound too good to be true (for example, God's free gift of salvation, forgiveness of sins, and eternal life with Him in heaven), false prophets tend to make claims that simply affirm our sinful nature. The Bible is a handy resource to test the claims of false teachers, because God never contradicts Himself.

Are you worried about spreading misinformation, either socially or spiritually? Men of purpose test every word against the truth before sharing it with others.

---

*Do you verify facts before sharing them?*
*Do you diligently consult the Bible*
*while listening to your preacher?*

# BE THE MAN WHO
# SEES THE BIG PICTURE

*"Don't store up treasures here on earth, where moths
eat them and rust destroys them, and where thieves
break in and steal. Store your treasures in heaven,
where moths and rust cannot destroy, and thieves
do not break in and steal. Wherever your treasure is,
there the desires of your heart will also be."*
MATTHEW 6:19–21 NLT

---

In the 1960s, Dr. Walter Mischel conducted a psychological experiment known as the "marshmallow test." The experiment was designed to test how a child's self-control might affect later life outcomes. Children were placed in a room with a marshmallow (or a cookie, pretzel, or other candy in later experiments) and told if they could resist the temptation to eat it for a certain amount of time, they'd get a second treat. Mischel's team then followed a few of these children through the years and found that those who waited were more likely to have successful futures.

In a 2018 study based on Mischel's research, Dr.

Tyler W. Watts varied the sample of children to include less-privileged households, better matching the racial and economic makeup of the United States' population. While there was still an indication that delayed gratification led to higher test scores in adolescence, many more factors impacted their success in later life.

Delayed gratification isn't a shortcut to success, but it is the first step. Matthew 6:20 encourages us to store up treasures in heaven to enjoy later, instead of treasures on earth, which will pass away. Mark 8:36 (NLT) sums it up this way: "And what do you benefit if you gain the whole world but lose your own soul?"

If we're part of God's family, our soul is secure. But without an eternal perspective, we'll accumulate our treasures in the wrong place. Our lives on earth are just a blip on eternity's radar, so we should have no problem using our current resources to bring others to God. We're not striving for another marshmallow. We're striving for real, eternal rewards!

---

*How does an eternal perspective help you make better daily decisions? How good are you at delayed gratification?*

# BE THE MAN WHO MEMORIZES SCRIPTURE

*Thy word have I hid in mine heart,*
*that I might not sin against thee.*
PSALM 119:11 KJV

In the Internet Age, the need to memorize has decreased significantly. Why commit things to memory when you can find them on your smartphone? While memorizing trivial facts may be a waste of time, hiding God's Word in our hearts is not. By memorizing scripture, we become more like the Author Himself.

But how do we do it? What's the best method for memorization?

According to Michael Nielsen—an Australian quantum physicist, science writer, and computer programming researcher—the answer is simple: flash cards.

The concept of spaced repetition—taking a break between learning sessions to better recall the information later—may not be new, but it's still effective.

Over Twitter, Nielsen said, "The use of spaced repetition memory systems has changed my life over the past couple of years. Here's a few things I've found helpful: I've memorized about 9,000, over 2 years. The single biggest change is that memory is no longer a haphazard event, to be left to chance. Rather, I can guarantee I will remember something, with minimal effort: it makes memory a choice.

"Rule of thumb: if memorizing something will likely save me five minutes in the future, into the spaced repetition system it goes."

The next time you're sipping coffee, eating lunch, or waiting for a meeting to start, use the time to memorize scripture. The more you get into God's Word, the more God's Word gets into you. And the more that happens, the less you'll be tempted to sin because you'll be looking at the world through God's truth.

---

*What verses have you already memorized? How can remembering God's Word help you avoid sin?*

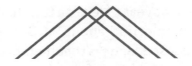

# BE THE MAN WHO CONTENDS FOR THE FAITH

*Dear friends, although I was very eager to write to you about the salvation we share, I felt compelled to write and urge you to contend for the faith that was once for all entrusted to God's holy people.*

JUDE 3 NIV

---

*Contend* isn't a word you hear every day. It means "to fight, compete, or engage in rivalry." It comes from the Latin word *contendere*, a word that combines "with" and "to stretch." If you've ever seen a wrestling match, you've seen what it means to contend.

Jude, the half brother of Jesus, urged all believers to contend for the faith, to fight for Christianity. Fighting isn't usually considered a Christian ideal. After all, Jesus says in Matthew 5:38–39 (NIV), "You have heard that it was said, 'Eye for eye, and tooth for tooth.' But I tell you, do not resist an evil person. If anyone slaps you on the right cheek, turn to them the other cheek also."

However, when it came to defending the faith,

Jesus was no pacifist. John 2:13–16 (NIV) says, "When it was almost time for the Jewish Passover, Jesus went up to Jerusalem. In the temple courts he found people selling cattle, sheep and doves, and others sitting at tables exchanging money. So he made a whip out of cords, and drove all from the temple courts, both sheep and cattle; he scattered the coins of the money changers and overturned their tables. To those who sold doves he said, 'Get these out of here! Stop turning my Father's house into a market!'"

When evil people persecute us, we should always turn the other cheek. But when false teachers or corrupt spiritual leaders attack our belief in Christ, it is our duty as men of purpose to fight back with truth, actively contending for our faith.

---

*What do you do when you hear someone who claims to be a Christian speaking lies about the faith? How can you know when someone is teaching falsely?*

## BE THE MAN
## WHO IS CONTENT

*Not that I was ever in need, for I have learned how to
be content with whatever I have. I know how to live
on almost nothing or with everything. I have learned
the secret of living in every situation, whether it is
with a full stomach or empty, with plenty or little.*
PHILIPPIANS 4:11–12 NLT

Contentment flies in the face of the American dream,
in which citizens are encouraged to always want more.
But with nearly 80 percent of American workers living
paycheck to paycheck (according to a 2017 survey by
CareerBuilder), contentment is a necessity.

In his letter to the Philippian church, the apostle
Paul writes, "For I can do everything through Christ,
who gives me strength" (Philippians 4:13 NLT). While
this verse is often misquoted as an inspirational saying by people reaching for some new dream, in its
biblical context, it describes how we can be content.

A man of purpose is satisfied living for God's glory,
sustained by God's strength. God doesn't promise

full stomachs, full wallets, or full health. Contentment has nothing to do with physical comforts; it has everything to do with spiritual reliance on the God who controls all things.

When Paul asked God to remove the thorn in the flesh that troubled him, God didn't do it. Second Corinthians 12:9 (NLT) says, "Each time he said, 'My grace is all you need. My power works best in weakness.' So now I am glad to boast about my weaknesses, so that the power of Christ can work through me."

Paul learned contentment in times of hardship, not in times of plenty. God has promised to give us strength and grace, not health and wealth, so our contentment and reliance on Him should never waver. When we do everything through Christ, we can boast in our weaknesses and be strong in God's power.

---

*What are some of the blessings God's given you?*
*How content are you with your situation?*

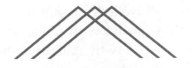

# BE THE MAN WHO LEARNS FROM MISTAKES

*As a dog returns to its vomit,*
*so fools repeat their folly.*
PROVERBS 26:11 NIV

According to the American Kennel Club, a dog's sense of smell is far keener than a human's, but their sense of taste is roughly one-sixth as powerful as ours. So when a dog finds something that smells like food, they eat it—even if it's vomit. They still taste it, but they don't seem to mind. In fact, it may remind them of their puppyhood.

As puppies are weaned off their mother's milk, they learn to eat regurgitated food. Since it's partially digested already, it's easier for their bodies to handle. Eating vomit may be disgusting for us, but for dogs, it's natural.

In Proverbs 26:11, the Bible compares a dog eating vomit to fools coming back to their folly. It's a good comparison. Folly comes naturally to fools.

King David wrote in Psalm 51:5 (NIV), "Surely I

was sinful at birth, sinful from the time my mother conceived me."

Though we naturally sin in our youth, we were never meant to stay there. Ephesians 2:3–5 (NIV) says, "All of us also lived among them at one time, gratifying the cravings of our flesh and following its desires and thoughts. Like the rest, we were by nature deserving of wrath. But because of his great love for us, God, who is rich in mercy, made us alive with Christ even when we were dead in transgressions—it is by grace you have been saved."

Sadly, many of us digest sin all too easily. Deadening our spiritual taste buds, we crave the things of the flesh. A man of purpose allows God to sharpen his palate so he doesn't confuse vomit for nourishing food. Folly may be natural for fools, but it's disgusting among God's children.

---

*Is there a specific sin you are still tempted by? How can you sharpen your palate for God's nourishment?*

# BE THE MAN
# WHO FORGIVES

*And be ye kind one to another, tenderhearted,*
*forgiving one another, even as God for*
*Christ's sake hath forgiven you.*
EPHESIANS 4:32 KJV

After a burp or similar bodily function, it is polite to say "Excuse me" or "Pardon me" if others are present. But why? Is there a difference between the two phrases?

Although the phrases are often used interchangeably, they point to different situations. To pardon implies forgiving someone who is guilty; to excuse implies recognizing someone's innocence.

The difference is one of responsibility. If a belch is truly unavoidable, "Excuse me" would be acceptable. But if you were showing off, saying "Pardon me" would be more appropriate.

Body functions may blur the line between excuses and pardons, but sin is never to be excused. When we choose ourselves over God's priorities, we sin (see Romans 2:6–9). When we know the right thing to do but don't do it, we sin (see James 4:17). Whether by commission or omission, our sins are not unavoidable situations (see 1 Corinthians 10:13).

Our sin does not require an excuse. It requires a pardon, which is exactly what God offers. He didn't pretend we were all right—He saw our sin and made a way for us to be forgiven.

When we accept Jesus' sacrifice, we experience God's pardon. When other people have wronged us, we need to pardon them too (see Ephesians 4:32). Forgiveness isn't excusing someone's behavior or pretending it didn't happen; it is choosing to leave the punishment up to God.

---

*Do you accept responsibility for your sins? If God has forgiven you, how can you better forgive others?*

# BE THE MAN WHO
# WORKS HARD

*Whatever you do, work at it with all your heart,
as working for the Lord, not for human masters.*
Colossians 3:23 niv

---

Slavery was common in ancient Colossae. Unlike slavery in the American South—in which skin color was the deciding factor—Roman slaves might have entered into servitude as a result of war. Or they might have sold themselves into slavery to pay off a debt.

The terms *slave*, *servant*, and *bondservant* all refer to individuals who are owned by their master, and Jesus used this form of servitude as an illustration of how Christians should live.

"Sitting down, Jesus called the Twelve and said, 'Anyone who wants to be first must be the very last, and the servant of all'" (Mark 9:35 niv).

Far from endorsing slavery, Jesus was encouraging believers to recognize their relationship to God the Father as their owner. Since God owns us, we are to love Him above all else and love our neighbors as ourselves (see Mark 12:30–31). How do we love our neighbors? By becoming a servant to all.

Paul carries the image further in Colossians 3, where he lays out instructions for members of a Christian household.

"Slaves, obey your earthly masters in everything; and do it, not only when their eye is on you and to curry their favor, but with sincerity of heart and reverence for the Lord. Whatever you do, work at it with all your heart, as working for the Lord, not for human masters, since you know that you will receive an inheritance from the Lord as a reward. It is the Lord Christ you are serving" (Colossians 3:22–24 NIV).

Being a man of purpose means recognizing your true Master and working accordingly.

---

*Are you a hard worker? Are you working for yourself or your Father in heaven?*

# BE THE MAN WHO DEFENDS THE OPPRESSED

*Learn to do right; seek justice. Defend the oppressed. Take up the cause of the fatherless; plead the case of the widow.*
ISAIAH 1:17 NIV

---

Oppression isn't a trivial matter, and ignoring it won't make it go away. Oppression is the antithesis of justice and thus one of the primary objects of God's wrath. As men of purpose, we must oppose it head-on.

What is oppression? It is the unjust exercise of authority by one person or group to keep another at a disadvantage. While oppression can be clearly seen in the schoolyard bully who steals kids' lunch money, it can also take the more insidious form of a rigged game that pretends to be fair, allowing everyone an equal opportunity to participate.

In the Old Testament, God spoke through His prophet Isaiah, calling His people to repent from doing evil and to start doing right. They were to stop playing rigged games and start defending the victims instead.

In the New Testament, James 1:27 (NIV) says, "Religion that God our Father accepts as pure and faultless is this: to look after orphans and widows in their distress and to keep oneself from being polluted by the world."

Widows and orphans held no power in ancient Israel. They had limited opportunities to improve their situations. Today, widows and orphans are protected by law, but many other groups are not. God still loves these people, and He still demands that those in authority give them justice.

This is where the enemy might whisper, "They have the same opportunities as you; they're just lazy," or "If God wanted them to be better off, He'd provide for them Himself," or "Giving preference to the oppressed is just another form of injustice."

Don't believe the lies. It's time for men in authority to stop benefiting from injustice and start defending the oppressed, no matter the cost.

---

*What privileges do you enjoy that others do not? How can you use your privileges to defend the oppressed?*

# BE THE MAN WHO KILLS RUMORS

*Fire goes out without wood, and quarrels*
*disappear when gossip stops.*
PROVERBS 26:20 NLT

---

The ability to build a roaring fire isn't a prerequisite for manliness, but there is something inherently testosterone-enhancing about setting a carefully stacked pile of wood ablaze.

However, whether your ideal campfire starts as a "tepee" (dry tinder in the center, pencil-thin kindling arranged in a cone around the tinder, with forearm-sized pieces of fuel wood on the outermost layer) or a "log cabin" (dry tinder and kindling arranged tepee-style, with fuel wood stacked in a square around it like large Lincoln Logs), there won't be much of a fire without wood.

The same is true for rumors. Remove the fuel and the rumor dies. Stop repeating what you've heard from others, and gossip will cease.

James 1:26 (NLT) says, "If you claim to be religious

but don't control your tongue, you are fooling yourself, and your religion is worthless."

It isn't enough to idly listen while someone spouts rumors to us—a man of purpose douses the flames of gossip with the water of truth. Listening to gossip only adds fuel. When others tell you a story about someone else, tell them you'd rather hear it from the source. Tell them it isn't right to talk about people behind their back. Tell them if they can't control their tongues, you'll have to avoid them altogether.

If someone gossips to you about others, they probably gossip to others about you. Proverbs 20:19 (NIV) says, "A gossip betrays a confidence; so avoid anyone who talks too much."

There's nothing manly about stoking the fires of gossip. Instead, speak the truth in love. Build an actual bonfire, inviting your friends over to discuss things openly. Lead by example. Kindle camaraderie, not rumors.

---

*How can social media be used to quench gossip, not fuel it? Have you ever betrayed someone's confidence by spreading rumors?*

# BE THE MAN WHO SHINES FROM THE HILLTOP

*Let your light so shine before men,
that they may see your good works,
and glorify your Father which is in heaven.*
MATTHEW 5:16 KJV

When Jesus gave the Sermon on the Mount, He used the geographical features of the land to impart God's truth.

In Matthew 5:14–16 (KJV) Jesus says, "Ye are the light of the world. A city that is set on an hill cannot be hid. Neither do men light a candle, and put it under a bushel, but on a candlestick; and it giveth light unto all that are in the house. Let your light so shine before men, that they may see your good works, and glorify your Father which is in heaven."

The ancient city of Hippos sat on a hill toward the southeastern end of the Sea of Galilee. As one of the cities of the Decapolis, Hippos was a Greco-Roman cultural center. Also, due to its naturally advantageous position, the city was fortified as a military outpost and would have been difficult to conquer. In fact, it took an earthquake, centuries after Christ walked the earth, to finally destroy it.

When Jesus compared His followers to a city on a hill, His original audience would have immediately thought of Hippos. Its position was obvious, and that was part of its strength.

A man of purpose draws strength from his identity in Christ, and his faith is made obvious by his actions. As Hippos was a cultural center for Greeks and Romans, Christians should live as cultural centers for God's values, representing Him in regions surrounded by other beliefs.

As children of God, we live on a hilltop, shining God's light through our good works. When we engage in ungodly deeds, we cover His light and rob Him of glory.

---

*Are you shining God's light or covering it up? How can you let your light shine more brightly before others?*

# BE THE MAN WHO PULLS HIS WEIGHT

*For even when we were with you,
we gave you this rule: "The one who
is unwilling to work shall not eat."*
2 THESSALONIANS 3:10 NIV

---

Work is not a consequence of sin. Genesis 2:15 (NIV) says, "The LORD God took the man and put him in the Garden of Eden to work it and take care of it."

Thorns are a result of sin (see Genesis 3:17–19), but work itself is good. However, since work is often difficult, some people refuse to do it. While many people are truly unable to work, inability and unwillingness are two vastly different things.

In his letters to the church at Thessalonica, Paul taught the value of hard work in this fallen world, and he led by example. He says in 1 Thessalonians 2:9 (NIV), "Surely you remember, brothers and sisters, our toil and hardship; we worked night and day in order not to be a burden to anyone while we preached the gospel of God to you."

Paul also called out those unwilling to follow his example. In 2 Thessalonians 3:6 (NIV) he writes, "In the name of the Lord Jesus Christ, we command you, brothers and sisters, to keep away from every believer who is idle and disruptive and does not live according to the teaching you received from us."

If we allow others to provide for us while refusing to pull our own weight, we abuse their kindness, portraying Christianity as a haven for laziness. Our hard work has no effect on our salvation, but our salvation should inspire us to work hard.

Hard work is an honorable thing. In the garden of your life, work the soil by the sweat of your brow. . .and God's seeds of love and faithfulness will grow in you.

---

*What do you like most about your work?*
*How can you pray for a better mindset*
*about the work you dislike?*

# BE THE MAN WHO HOLDS BACK ANGER

*Fools vent their anger, but the
wise quietly hold it back.*
PROVERBS 29:11 NLT

Getting cut off in traffic. . .being held up in the grocery aisle. . .sitting next to a talker in the theater. We all have things that make us angry.

Being angry, in itself, isn't sin. How we deal with anger could be, though.

Proverbs 29:11 (NLT) says, "Fools vent their anger, but the wise quietly hold it back." This doesn't mean we should always swallow our anger—that just causes an ulcer. It means we shouldn't let rage rule our actions.

"Think before you speak" is more than good parental advice. It's the top anger management tip in an article by the Mayo Clinic. Second on the list is "Once you're calm, express your anger."

These tips fit well with what the Bible teaches. Ecclesiastes 7:9 (NLT) says, "Control your temper, for anger labels you a fool." And Ephesians 4:26–27 (NLT) says, " 'Don't sin by letting anger control you.' Don't let the sun go down while you are still angry, for anger gives a foothold to the devil."

It's healthy to take a moment to calm down when we're riled. But when we try to ignore what's bothering us, we do more harm than good. It's always best to address our anger while we still remember what we are angry about.

Men of purpose deal with their frustration in healthy ways, knowing that God will bring justice in the end. You can trust Him and let go of your anger, or your anger will lead you to sin. The choice is yours.

---

*What makes you angry? How can you address your anger and give it to God?*

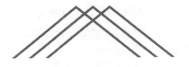

# BE THE MAN WHO TRUSTS GOD

*Trust in the LORD with all thine heart; and lean not unto thine own understanding. In all thy ways acknowledge him, and he shall direct thy paths.*
PROVERBS 3:5–6 KJV

---

Have you ever bought a new bottle of ketchup to replace the one you couldn't find, only to find the old one immediately afterward? The inability to see things right in front of us is, sadly, one of the things men are known for. But science may have an answer that explains why.

"What we pay attention to is largely determined by our expectations of what should be present," says Christopher Chabris, a cognitive psychologist who coauthored *The Invisible Gorilla*.

The title of Chabris's book is inspired by a YouTube video that instructs its viewers to count the number of times a basketball is passed between people wearing white shirts. While the viewers are focusing on the basketball, most completely miss the man in a gorilla suit who walks across the screen.

As Chabris notes in his book, our minds don't work the way we think they do. Without expecting something, we're unlikely to pay attention to it, he says, and "when we are not paying attention to something, we are surprisingly likely to not see it."

It is no wonder, then, that the Bible tells us not to lean on our own understanding. If we can miss ketchup bottles and gorillas that are right in front of us, we can also overlook God's guidance in our life. But as Chabris noted, when we learn to pay better attention and discount our assumptions, we'll be better prepared to see things as they truly are.

Men of purpose trust God more than their own viewpoint. We must acknowledge Him in order to see what is true and what He wants for us.

---

*Have your expectations ever altered your perspective? How can you better trust God's viewpoint over your own?*

# BE THE MAN WHO HATES EVIL

*Hate evil and love what is good; turn your courts into true halls of justice. Perhaps even yet the LORD God of Heaven's Armies will have mercy on the remnant of his people.*

AMOS 5:15 NLT

---

Murder is evil—there's not much debate about that. But is it evil to simply wish someone were dead? Adultery is wrong. But how wrong is it to fantasize about someone other than your wife? When it comes to right and wrong, we tend to visualize things on a spectrum. We think of murder as worse than hatred and adultery as worse than viewing pornography.

The truth is less nuanced than we'd like to think. Sin is sin, even when it pretends to be harmless.

In Matthew 5:21–22 (NLT), Jesus says, "You have heard that our ancestors were told, 'You must not murder. If you commit murder, you are subject to judgment.' But I say, if you are even angry with someone, you are subject to judgment! If you call someone an idiot, you are in danger of being brought before the court. And if you curse someone, you are in danger of the fires of hell."

And in Matthew 5:27–28 (NLT), He adds, "You have heard the commandment that says, 'You must not commit adultery.' But I say, anyone who even looks at a woman with lust has already committed adultery with her in his heart."

Until we start viewing sin as evil—not on a spectrum but as its own category—we will not hate it as we should. Men of purpose understand that to downplay sin is evil in itself. The effects of sin are devastating and nothing about it is redeemable. That is why we needed to be rescued from sin instead of merely redirected toward good.

---

*Do you hate evil? How can your actions and attitude show your views on good versus evil?*

# BE THE MAN WHO
# LOVES HIS NEIGHBOR

*"The most important one," answered Jesus,*
*"is this: 'Hear, O Israel: The Lord our God,*
*the Lord is one. Love the Lord your God with*
*all your heart and with all your soul and with*
*all your mind and with all your strength.' The*
*second is this: 'Love your neighbor as yourself.'*
*There is no commandment greater than these."*
MARK 12:29–31 NIV

A neighbor is someone who lives next door. . .or a million miles away. A neighbor is someone who mows your grass when you're away. . .or someone whose dog poops on your lawn. Everyone is your neighbor, whether you like them or not. You are called to love them all.

But since loving everyone all the time is a difficult concept to grasp, let's focus on our literal neighbors for now. If no one lives directly next to you, think of acquaintances with whom you regularly interact. How can you love these people?

The first step is knowing their names. If you've lived next to them for so long that asking their name is embarrassing, get over it. A man of purpose swallows his pride to love his neighbor. If you need an excuse to ask your neighbor's name, bring a gift, explaining how you would like to be a better neighbor.

The second step is to see your neighbors as people, ignoring the annoying things they might do. They might be the type who revs their truck engine after bedtime; if so, find common ground by asking them about their truck's make and model, for instance.

The third step is finding ways to serve them. Think of Jesus' parable about the Good Samaritan (see Luke 10:25–37 if you need a refresher). In this story, the good neighbor is the one who serves the needs of the injured traveler. We are to serve in the same way.

Once you master loving your actual neighbor, see how you can grow your neighborhood.

---

*How can you get to know your neighbors better? How can you serve them?*

# BE THE MAN WHO PRAISES OTHERS

*Do not withhold good from those to whom
it is due, when it is in your power to act.*
PROVERBS 3:27 NIV

Doing a job well feels better when someone praises you for it. Whether you've nailed a presentation at work, baked the perfect loaf of bread, or caught a fish the size of a Buick, it means more when someone notices. And yet, we sometimes choose to withhold praise from those who have earned it.

Why? Maybe we're too wrapped up in ourselves to see the achievements of others. Or maybe we don't want to draw attention to their accomplishments for fear that our own won't measure up.

As men of purpose, we are called to praise what is praiseworthy, being kind whenever possible. Proverbs 3:27 (NIV) says, "Do not withhold good from those to whom it is due, when it is in your power to act."

Praising the accomplishments of others reveals things about you too: You value expertise. You're detail oriented. You're a positive person. You share your opinions, making it easier for others to share their opinions with you.

Of course, you should never give someone false praise or withhold constructive criticism. Proverbs 27:6 (NIV) says, "Wounds from a friend can be trusted, but an enemy multiplies kisses."

When we compliment someone, it should be true, helpful, and genuine. The same three characteristics apply to criticisms as well. The difference is that praise should be given freely in public, but criticism should be reserved solely for the person with whom we find fault.

If you're pleased when people notice the good things you do, be the man who notices the accomplishments of others. Always be ready to say, "Good job."

---

*When was the last time you gave someone a compliment? What are some qualities you appreciate about someone else?*

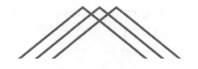

# BE THE MAN WHO
# BEARS FRUIT

*But the Holy Spirit produces this kind of fruit*
*in our lives: love, joy, peace, patience, kindness,*
*goodness, faithfulness, gentleness, and self-control.*
*There is no law against these things!*
GALATIANS 5:22–23 NLT

---

Apple trees and pear trees are both members of the Rosaceae family of plants. Both can exceed twenty feet in height, and both produce edible fruits. Want to know how to tell them apart? Look at the fruit. Apple trees produce apples. Pear trees produce pears.

Want to know how to tell Christians from non-Christians? The same way: Look at their fruit.

Galatians 5:19–23 (NLT) explains the difference this way: "When you follow the desires of your sinful nature, the results are very clear: sexual immorality, impurity, lustful pleasures, idolatry, sorcery, hostility, quarreling, jealousy, outbursts of anger, selfish ambition, dissension, division, envy, drunkenness, wild parties, and other sins like these. Let me tell you again, as I have before, that anyone living that sort of life will not inherit the Kingdom of God.

"But the Holy Spirit produces this kind of fruit in our lives: love, joy, peace, patience, kindness, goodness, faithfulness, gentleness, and self-control. There is no law against these things!"

In Matthew 12:33 (NLT), Jesus says, "A tree is identified by its fruit. If a tree is good, its fruit will be good. If a tree is bad, its fruit will be bad."

Before you start examining other people's fruit though, remember God is the fruit inspector, not us. He is the farmer who cultivates the soil, and we must be willing to allow Him to work in us. When we submit to God, we'll start bearing the right kind of fruit.

Jesus, in John 15:5 (NLT), says, "Yes, I am the vine; you are the branches. Those who remain in me, and I in them, will produce much fruit. For apart from me you can do nothing."

---

*Do you exhibit sinful fruit or the fruit of the Spirit? How might you allow God to cultivate spiritual fruit in your life?*

# BE THE MAN WHO EXHIBITS EMOTIONAL INTELLIGENCE

*Rejoice with them that do rejoice,
and weep with them that weep.*
ROMANS 12:15 KJV

Feelings aren't your enemy. Some men just don't know what to do with them. Psychologist Marc Brackett—founder of the Yale Center for Emotional Intelligence and author of *Permission to Feel*—says avoiding emotions can be disastrous.

To begin properly facing our feelings, we can employ the system Brackett developed to teach emotional intelligence skills in schools: R.U.L.E.R.

- *Recognize*: The first step toward dealing with emotions is to recognize we have them. When a situation raises your hackles, don't shrug it off. Whenever you feel sad, happy, anxious, or serene, embrace it.
- *Understand*: Once you recognize an emotion, look for clues as to why you are feeling it. What just happened? Are your feelings connected

to a similar past experience? Sorting out your feelings may take time and serious effort. Be patient.

- *Label*: Discard the words *good* and *bad* as descriptions of how you're feeling. Expand your vocabulary. Get specific. In *Permission to Feel*, Brackett writes, "We know from neuroscience and brain imaging research that there is real, tangible truth to the proposition that 'if you can name it, you can tame it.'"

- *Express*: This is where many men fail, either by hiding their feelings or by expressing them in the wrong way at the wrong time. It's important to find someone trustworthy to confide in, preventing our feelings from piling up.

- *Regulate*: Emotional regulation is a way to control your feelings so they don't control you. Pray for the people who irritate you. Learn to avoid engaging people who only want to fight.

As men of purpose, we must embrace emotions and deal with them intelligently. Then we can better reflect God's patience and understanding to the world around us.

---

*How emotionally intelligent are you? On which area of the R.U.L.E.R. system can you improve?*

# BE THE MAN WHO STRIVES FOR PERFECTION

*"But you are to be perfect, even as your Father in heaven is perfect."*
MATTHEW 5:48 NLT

---

In the Sermon on the Mount, Jesus set new guidelines for living holy lives. Instead of simply refraining from murder, for instance, we are to reject hate altogether. Likewise, we are to love our enemies, go the extra mile for others, and even gouge out our eyes if they tempt us to lust. Jesus wasn't messing around!

This section of the sermon concludes with a seemingly impossible task: "But you are to be perfect, even as your Father in heaven is perfect" (Matthew 5:48 NLT).

Men of purpose don't get easy passes. Jesus was serious about perfection and, fortunately for us, explained exactly how to get there.

Matthew 19:16–30 tells the story of a rich man who claimed to have followed the Hebrew law to the letter, yet knew he was still missing something.

In Matthew 19:21 (NLT) Jesus tells him, "If you want to be perfect, go and sell all your possessions and give the money to the poor, and you will have treasure in heaven. Then come, follow me."

By human standards, the rich man was pretty close to perfection. But Jesus revealed the one thing standing in the way: this man's wealth meant more to him than following Jesus.

The only way to be perfect is to give up whatever stands in the way of following Jesus—because Jesus is the only perfect sacrifice for our sins. If riches are holding you back, sell everything and give the money to God. If you're gripped by pride, humble yourself in your own eyes first, then crawl to Christ on your knees.

Perfection is possible only through Jesus. We are called to forsake everything that stands between us and Him.

---

*Is anything standing between you and Christ? If so, how can you lay it down at Jesus' feet?*

# BE THE MAN WHO FIGHTS RACISM

*There is neither Jew nor Greek, there is neither bond nor free, there is neither male nor female: for ye are all one in Christ Jesus.*
GALATIANS 3:28 KJV

---

Racism is a touchy subject for many, Christians included. The church hasn't always been on the right side of issues like slavery and inclusion, but Christ came to seek the lost and unite all people under the banner of His love. All people, regardless of race, ethnicity, or skin color, are made in the image of God and deserve to be treated as such.

Jemar Tisby, author of *How to Fight Racism*, writes this: "Each people group with their various languages, dress, foods, clothing, and customs reveals a finite facet of God's infinite diversity. The kingdom of God is described as a banquet to which all, especially those on society's margins, are invited (Luke 14). Perhaps this banquet will be a potluck. Ethiopians will bring injera, Nigerians jollof, Jamaicans goat curry, and

Koreans kimchee. Like a communal banquet that highlights the best aspects of different cultures, the heavenly congregation will put on display the magnificent diversity of God's people."

By recognizing the diverse nature of God in people who are unlike ourselves, we can more fully appreciate the image of God. No single racial or ethnic group can fully display God's glory by themselves.

Christianity is where the walls of racism are meant to fall. Ephesians 2:13–14 (NLT) says, "But now you have been united with Christ Jesus. Once you were far away from God, but now you have been brought near to him through the blood of Christ. For Christ himself has brought peace to us. He united Jews and Gentiles into one people when, in his own body on the cross, he broke down the wall of hostility that separated us."

Men of purpose fight racism by recognizing the image of God in others and welcoming all to the diverse banquet of God's love.

---

*How do you view people from other racial or ethnic backgrounds? How can you build relationships with people unlike yourself?*

# BE THE MAN WHO WORKS
# OUT HIS SALVATION

*Therefore, my dear friends, as you have always
obeyed—not only in my presence, but now much more
in my absence—continue to work out your salvation
with fear and trembling, for it is God who works in you
to will and to act in order to fulfill his good purpose.*
PHILIPPIANS 2:12–13 NIV

In his letter to the Philippians, Paul encouraged Christians to work out their salvation with fear and trembling. That's a pretty confusing thing to say.

First John 4:18 (NIV) says, "There is no fear in love. But perfect love drives out fear, because fear has to do with punishment. The one who fears is not made perfect in love."

Is Paul suggesting we should be afraid because our salvation isn't sure? Doesn't salvation involve recognizing God's perfect love for us?

Let's think about it another way.

Athletes work out. They don't work for a new body; they work the bodies they have. They train their bodies through exercise, shedding fat and building muscle while being careful of what they consume. They are motivated by an internal desire that overpowers their desire to eat junk food and be lazy.

Similarly, Christians don't work for salvation. There's nothing we can do to earn God's love (see Ephesians 2:8–9). We train our minds and hearts through spiritual exercise, shedding sinful choices and building love for others while being careful of what we consume. We're motivated by something stronger than a desire to be healthy. Philippians 2:13 says it is God who works in us, motivating us to fulfill His good purpose.

The fear and trembling we experience while we "work out" our salvation is simply our recognition of God living within us. We don't fear God's wrath—Jesus has already taken our punishment—but we do treat God's presence with the respect and gravity He deserves.

In exercising our spiritual muscles for others, we strengthen our relationship with God, fulfilling His will in our lives.

---

*How are you working out your salvation? What is a spiritual exercise you could improve on?*

# BE THE MAN WHO VALUES MENTORSHIP

*In the same way, encourage the young men to live wisely. And you yourself must be an example to them by doing good works of every kind. Let everything you do reflect the integrity and seriousness of your teaching. Teach the truth so that your teaching can't be criticized. Then those who oppose us will be ashamed and have nothing bad to say about us.*
TITUS 2:6–8 NLT

How do men learn? Some men read instructional books. Some learn through trial and error. One of the best ways to learn, however, is to watch someone who knows what he's doing.

Not only does learning from someone else's experience apply to fixing cars and grilling hamburgers, it applies to the Christian life.

A man of purpose seeks out experienced Christians to share their wisdom.

Older guys, it is your duty to seek out younger guys who might benefit from your wisdom. If you think you don't know how or what to teach, just stick to sharing what you've learned from the Bible. If you stick to the truth, no one can second-guess you.

Younger guys, seek out those who have been where you want to be. Ask them to share their experiences with you. Ask them how they reached that point and what truths they live by daily.

Mentorships can be as lax or as formal as you'd like, but a few ground rules will help them go better. First, discuss your hopes for what the mentorship will look like. How often will you meet? Will you meet by phone, by video call, or in person? What kind of information are you hoping to learn from each other? Yes, this is a two-way deal.

Second, be honest with one another. There's nothing to be gained from sharing false information.

Third, be gracious with each other. As with any relationship, there will be miscommunications and mistakes. Fortunately, as Christian men, we can rally around the fact that God has forgiven us, making it possible (and required) for us to forgive each other.

---

*Do you know someone who could benefit from your experience, or vice versa? How can you touch base with that person this week?*

# BE THE MAN WHO PRAISES GOD

*Praise the LORD, all you nations;*
*extol him, all you peoples. For great is*
*his love toward us, and the faithfulness of*
*the LORD endures forever. Praise the LORD.*
PSALM 117 NIV

---

Psalm 117 is the shortest chapter in the Bible, but its message is all-encompassing. The substance is simple, beginning and ending with "Praise the LORD."

Why is God praiseworthy? Because of His great love for us. While many psalms sing of either personal matters or Israel's specific needs, Psalm 117 is a chorus for the whole world to sing. The "us" in the psalm refers to everyone. God loves us all, and His faithfulness to us endures forever.

God proved His love by sending His Son to die for the whole world (see John 3:16). First Corinthians 1:9 (NIV) says, "God is faithful, who has called you into fellowship with his Son, Jesus Christ our Lord."

When we have mountaintop experiences and are

keenly aware of God's presence, praising Him is easy. When we travel through the valley and feel far from God, we are still called to praise Him. Our feelings and moods do not change God's love or faithfulness. He is always worthy of praise.

In fact, it's more important to praise God when we feel distant because our focus will shift from ourselves to our Creator. Praising God opens a window from our present circumstance to the One who holds our future.

Need some tips for getting started? Psalm 103 offers a whole list: "Praise the LORD, my soul, and forget not all his benefits—who forgives all your sins and heals all your diseases, who redeems your life from the pit and crowns you with love and compassion, who satisfies your desires with good things so that your youth is renewed like the eagle's. The LORD works righteousness and justice for all the oppressed" (Psalm 103:2–6 NIV).

---

*What are some things to praise God for today? How has praising Him in the valley helped change your perspective?*

# BE THE MAN WHO
# DOESN'T COMPLAIN

*Do everything without complaining and arguing,
so that no one can criticize you. Live clean, innocent
lives as children of God, shining like bright lights in
a world full of crooked and perverse people.*
PHILIPPIANS 2:14–15 NLT

Not only is complaining useless in solving problems, it can often cause more. In a scientific study by Robert Sapolsky—professor of neurology and neuroendocrinology at Stanford University's School of Medicine—it was found that the negativity associated with complaining can actually damage a person's brain.

But if complaining is harmful, why do we keep doing it? Some people complain to relieve stress (ironic, given how much it stresses others out). Some people do it because it offers the illusion of action in a hopeless situation. Others complain because they learned the behavior in childhood.

Even when the reasons seem valid, complaining will not fix our problems or draw people to our cause.

The solution to complaining is surrender—not surrendering to the problem, but surrendering the problem to God.

When we give our worries to God, we forfeit the right to complain about them. We can claim the peace offered by Jesus in John 16:33 (NLT): "I have told you all this so that you may have peace in me. Here on earth you will have many trials and sorrows. But take heart, because I have overcome the world."

By surrendering our complaints, we recognize God's overwhelming ability to fix what we cannot. When we live without complaint, trusting God with our lives, we will shine as a positive example in a world of negativity.

---

*Are you guilty of complaining instead of trusting God? After surrendering your complaints to God, how can you prevent yourself from taking them back?*

# BE THE MAN WHO CALLS ON THE LORD WITH A PURE HEART

*Flee also youthful lusts: but follow righteousness, faith, charity, peace, with them that call on the Lord out of a pure heart.*
2 TIMOTHY 2:22 KJV

---

The word *pure* comes from the Latin *purus*, which means "clean, clear, or unmixed." In the context of a Christian life, calling on the Lord with a pure heart means coming to God with the whole of our being, not mixing our attention or affections with other things.

In the Old Testament, Moses warned the Israelites against mixing their worship of God with the worship of idols from surrounding nations. If they broke their vows of loyalty to Him in the Promised Land (as He knew they would), God gave them this warning: "There you will worship man-made gods of wood and stone, which cannot see or hear or eat or smell. But if from there you seek the LORD your God, you will find him if you seek him with all your heart and with all your soul" (Deuteronomy 4:28–29 NIV).

When the Israelites chased the wrong things, they found themselves in captivity. When they chased after God with pure hearts, they found Him.

Paul used the same formula when describing the Christian life to Timothy, his protégé. "Flee also youthful lusts: but follow righteousness, faith, charity, peace, with them that call on the Lord out of a pure heart" (2 Timothy 2:22 KJV).

It isn't enough to flee from sin. A man of purpose must actively pursue the things of God. We can't run after two different goals, mixing our worship of the Creator with the work of our own hands. We are to pursue righteousness, faith, charity, and peace. Fortunately, we aren't running alone; we are joined by every believer who calls on God with a pure heart.

---

*Are you chasing after God with a pure heart? How can you encourage fellow believers who run alongside you?*

# BE THE MAN WHO CHOOSES FRIENDS CAREFULLY

*Walk with the wise and become wise,*
*for a companion of fools suffers harm.*
PROVERBS 13:20 NIV

---

In a 2014 study about friendship, researchers Michael L. Lowe of Texas A&M University and Kelly L. Haws of Vanderbilt found that men who made decisions together deepened their friendship over time. If they made a good decision together, they bonded over their shared virtues. If they decided to participate in vice together, they bonded as partners in crime.

This study reveals an important truth about our decision-making process: Whether our goal is virtue or vice, we'll feel better about our decisions when they are made with friends. As men of purpose, it should be our goal to seek virtue, because the consequences of vice are always more severe than we think.

Proverbs 13:20 (NIV) says, "Walk with the wise and become wise, for a companion of fools suffers harm." And 1 Corinthians 15:33 (NIV) says, "Do not be misled: 'Bad company corrupts good character.'"

Our friends naturally influence us—for good or ill—so we must be wise in choosing them.

If you need to break off some old friendships that led you in the wrong direction, stop frequenting your old meeting-places and look for better relationships elsewhere. Churches are a great place to find friends with common values. Alternatively, pick a wholesome activity you enjoy and introduce yourself to the guys who do the same.

Friends are important—but friends who push you toward wisdom are irreplaceable.

---

*How do your friends inspire you to live?*
*How can you encourage your friends to be wise?*

# BE THE MAN WHO SHOWS HOSPITALITY

*Do not forget to show hospitality to strangers,*
*for by so doing some people have shown*
*hospitality to angels without knowing it.*
HEBREWS 13:2 NIV

---

Ovid was a Roman poet who lived in the time of Caesar Augustus, and his *Metamorphoses* is one of the most important sources of classical mythology. In book eight of the collection, we find the story of Baucis and Philemon.

In the tale, Jupiter and Mercury—the Roman counterparts to Zeus and Hermes—travel to the city of Tyana disguised as peasants. They are greeted only by locked doors and unkind words, coming at last to the cottage of Baucis and Philemon—a poor couple who treat their guests with respect and rich hospitality. When Baucis notices that her pitcher of wine gets no emptier when serving her guests and Philemon's attempt to kill the family goose results in the goose climbing into Jupiter's lap, the couple realize their guests are supernatural.

In a scene reminiscent of the biblical story of Lot, the gods inform Baucis and Philemon that Tyana is going to be destroyed for its lack of hospitality. The couple flee the town and watch from a safe distance as a flood washes it away.

Hospitality was important in antiquity. People genuinely believed they could be hosting supernatural guests, so they treated all guests well. In fact, Acts 14:8–18 tells the story of how the people of Lystra (not far from Tyana) mistook Paul and Barnabas for Hermes and Zeus and sought to honor them as such.

Even though we might shake our heads at the misunderstanding, the Bible encourages such hospitality. Hebrews 13:2 (NIV) says, "Do not forget to show hospitality to strangers, for by so doing some people have shown hospitality to angels without knowing it."

Being men of purpose means welcoming others into our home and treating them with the same respect we would a supernatural guest.

---

*How can you show hospitality to someone in need? When was the last time you hosted a stranger in your home?*

# BE THE MAN WHO ADMITS WHEN HE'S WRONG

*If we say that we have no sin, we deceive
ourselves, and the truth is not in us.*
1 JOHN 1:8 KJV

---

Exodus 20:16 (NIV) says, "You shall not give false testimony against your neighbor." This commandment is pretty simple. While the specific wording applies narrowly to situations involving neighbors and courtroom-style testimony, the broader rule of "Thou shalt not lie" is easily remembered and more applicable to our lives. Lying is wrong.

Does it matter who we're lying to? Or about?

Fyodor Dostoyevsky once said, "Lying to ourselves is more deeply ingrained than lying to others."

Self-deception is a perilous game that can take many forms:

- Simple denial: flatly saying something didn't happen or couldn't happen
- Reality distortion: remembering things differently than how they were

- Projection: attributing our feelings onto other people
- Idealization: downplaying the negatives and remembering the positives
- Rationalization: making excuses for our negative actions

Psychology reveals self-deception as a natural defense mechanism designed to keep us moving forward through life. The problem, however, is that it prevents us from truly experiencing God's love. We adopt a false identity, seeking love from the world instead of presenting our true selves before God and accepting His perfect love and forgiveness.

God's truth cannot dwell inside a false image of ourselves. The first step to recovery is admitting we have a problem. There's a reason the verse after 1 John 1:9 says, "If we confess our sins, he is faithful and just and will forgive us our sins and purify us from all unrighteousness" (NIV).

When we do wrong, we need to admit it to ourselves, to God, and to others. Only by confessing our sins can we enjoy true healing.

---

*Are you lying to yourself about anything? If so, what might be holding you back from the truth?*

# BE THE MAN WHO PERSEVERES

*Consider it pure joy, my brothers
and sisters, whenever you face trials
of many kinds, because you know that the
testing of your faith produces perseverance.
Let perseverance finish its work so that you may
be mature and complete, not lacking anything.*
JAMES 1:2–4 NIV

There are thousands of reasons not to exercise. Weather isn't always conducive. Our schedules might not allow for it. We don't want to cramp up after eating and potentially drown (sure, this only applies to swimming; it's best to play it safe).

And, according to a study that appears in *Men's Health* magazine, men who exercise rigorously even have a greater chance of dying!

But many of our "reasons" not to exercise are really excuses, right? Sure, we need to be careful not to overdo it, but many other studies have shown the greater danger lies in laziness and unhealthy diets.

The same is true with our spiritual health. We can

think of many "reasons" why we shouldn't share our faith or why we don't have time to read our Bible, but these are really excuses. James 1:2–3 called them "trials" or "tests."

Refusing to give in to temptations makes perseverance easier in the future. When we pass up a candy bar in favor of a walk around the block, for instance, the candy bar holds less temptation to us in the future. In both spiritual and physical trials, the goal is maturity.

Immature people have no self-control, but men of purpose see temptations as opportunities to overcome. In fact, choosing spiritual perseverance results in joy that no earthly reward could match.

---

*Where do you fall on the maturity scale?*
*What might you need to change*
*about your exercise habits?*

# BE THE MAN WHO VALUES TEAMWORK

*I appeal to you, brothers and sisters, in the name of our Lord Jesus Christ, that all of you agree with one another in what you say and that there be no divisions among you, but that you be perfectly united in mind and thought.*
1 CORINTHIANS 1:10 NIV

---

Think of the last great team you were on. Everyone got along, pulled their weight, and supported each other. Now think of the opposite kind of team—constant fighting, unequal workloads, and members constantly throwing each other under the bus. What sets these two types apart?

James Folkman, founder of two leadership development firms, once wrote an article for *Forbes* on what sets highly effective teams apart. According to Folkman, these team leaders

- inspire more than they drive
- help resolve conflicts quickly
- set stretch goals—audacious goals that can

only be accomplished by the specific team in question
- communicate vision and direction
- are trusted

These team leadership tips can all be found in the apostle Paul's example to the church of Corinth. After opening with inspiration (1 Corinthians 1:4–9), he moves on to an appeal for unity (1:10). His stretch goal is for church members to love each other perfectly (chapter 13). His vision is to clearly communicate the resurrection of Christ (15:1–5). And his trustworthiness lies in his own experience with Jesus (15:8–11).

Being a man of purpose means valuing teamwork and leading by example. You have the ability to make your team (your family, your workplace, your church) more dream than scream by following Paul's example.

Inspire others by praying for them and praising them. Address conflicts calmly yet openly, not allowing them to fester into behind-the-back bickering. Set a stretch goal for your team to achieve with you. Communicate your vision continuously. And be trustworthy in all your dealings.

---

*What are some of your best moments of teamwork? How can you avoid bad team experiences?*

# BE THE MAN WHO IS WISE WITH HIS EYES

*"But I say, anyone who even looks at a woman with lust has already committed adultery with her in his heart."*
MATTHEW 5:28 NLT

---

As official crime statistics continue to tick downward, the world should be safer than ever. In reality, the dangers are getting more subversive. Things that were once morally reprehensible are now shrugged off as normal parts of life. Sin is not frowned upon; it is winked at.

The internet has changed the way the world works. Businesses are global; meetings can be performed remotely; relationships begin on apps before people ever meet in person. And pornography is only a click away.

What used to be a private sin has become a public joke. Mainstream films and television shows use pornography as a punch line. According to a Gallup poll from 2018, 43 percent of Americans view pornography as morally acceptable, a figure 7 percent higher than the same poll from 2017. Is pornography really a big deal?

Jesus says it is.

In Matthew 5:27–29 (NLT), Jesus says, "You have heard the commandment that says, 'You must not commit adultery.' But I say, anyone who even looks at a woman with lust has already committed adultery with her in his heart. So if your eye—even your good eye—causes you to lust, gouge it out and throw it away. It is better for you to lose one part of your body than for your whole body to be thrown into hell."

Lust is the intentional viewing of someone else for the purpose of arousal, and Jesus makes it abundantly clear that it's a big deal. An eyeball-gouge-worthy big deal. Why? Because lust is a form of idolatry. Pornography twists God's design for sexuality into an object of worship, an outlet for our selfish desires.

Becoming a man of purpose means recognizing pornography as sin and treating it as such.

---

*Do you see pornography as acceptable?*
*How can you make sure you don't fall into its trap?*

# BE THE MAN WHO SEEKS UNDERSTANDING

*Fools have no interest in understanding;*
*they only want to air their own opinions.*
PROVERBS 18:2 NLT

---

Some guys treat communication like a one-way street. They see your contribution to the conversation as merely another opportunity for them to think of a reply. You can tell they're doing this whenever their response has nothing to do with what you just said. These people are terrible conversationalists, and the Bible calls them fools.

"Fools have no interest in understanding; they only want to air their own opinions" (Proverbs 18:2 NLT).

"Fools think their own way is right, but the wise listen to others" (Proverbs 12:15 NLT).

If two-way conversations are difficult for you, maybe your ears need a tune-up.

Proverbs 2:2 (NLT) says, "Tune your ears to wisdom, and concentrate on understanding."

A good way of showing others you are listening

is to concentrate on what they are saying and ignore your inner monologue.

Good listeners also ask questions based on what the speaker says. It's difficult to ask related questions if you don't listen. Requests for clarification or even repetition are acceptable. If you got lost in your thoughts, missing part of what the other person has said, be honest and ask for forgiveness. The reason someone is talking to you is because that person values you.

Don't be a fool when it comes to communication, especially when it's with God.

If our prayers are one-sided—if we ignore what God is trying to tell us—we are far from the wisdom and understanding He wants us to have. It's okay to apologize and ask God to repeat Himself. He wants you to understand His love and His will for your life.

---

*Do you consider yourself a good listener?*
*How might you improve your understanding?*

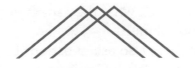

# BE THE MAN WHO DOES GOD'S WILL

*Rejoice always, pray continually, give thanks
in all circumstances; for this is God's
will for you in Christ Jesus.*
1 THESSALONIANS 5:16–18 NIV

---

God's will is perfect. His plans cannot be thwarted. Nothing can happen without His approval. If only we could be that certain about our own desires and plans. Or if only we knew for sure what He wants for us.

Should we find a new job or stick with the one we have? Do we take our relationship to the next level or cool things off for a bit? What should we make for dinner? Do we invest in the market or pay down our mortgage?

When faced with too many options, we quickly fall victim to decision fatigue. Scientists have discovered a correlation between the number of decisions a person makes and that person's likelihood of making poor or uninformed decisions. After a certain amount of choices, we become incapable of wise decisions.

While we might ponder what to make for dinner, we don't need to waste any mental energy figuring out God's will for our lives. He tells us exactly what to do in 1 Thessalonians 5:16–18 (NIV): "Rejoice always, pray continually, give thanks in all circumstances; for this is God's will for you in Christ Jesus."

Joy, prayer, and thanksgiving are to be the hallmarks of our lives. Being a man of purpose means actively choosing to rejoice in God's goodness, praying for God's wisdom, and giving thanks regardless of the circumstances.

When we trust God, joyfully putting our lives in His hands and thanking Him for whatever happens, He is free to perform His will through us. No decision fatigue required.

---

*How can you rearrange your schedule so your biggest decisions are made early in the day? Do you tend to make bad choices late at night when your willpower is low?*

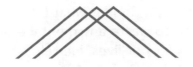

# BE THE MAN WHO LEAVES SIN IN THE TOMB

*Knowing this, that our old man is crucified with him, that the body of sin might be destroyed, that henceforth we should not serve sin. For he that is dead is freed from sin.*
Romans 6:6–7 KJV

What goes into a tomb should stay in a tomb. Jesus is the only notable exception to this rule. Everything else is the stuff of horror movies. Even worse are the true stories of people exhuming bodies for nefarious purposes—laws and common sense both tell us to leave dead bodies alone.

According to Numbers 19, anyone who touched a dead body or was in the same room as a dead body was ceremonially unclean for seven days. If the unclean person didn't partake in specific purification rituals, they were to be cut off from the rest of the community. That's a pretty serious punishment!

And yet, Christians who are dead to sin through Jesus' sacrifice still occasionally creep into sin's tomb.

If the thought of playing around with your decomposing sin doesn't gross you out, then you aren't taking redemption seriously enough.

Jesus died and rose again to give us new life, declaring us pure and freeing us from our tombs! Why on earth would we ever go back in?

Because, just like in a horror movie, sin's dead body doesn't want to release its hold on life. It calls to us, reminds us of the "fun" we used to have, and lies about the consequences. We have been rescued from ultimate destruction, but we lose our close community with God and His church when we return to the tomb of our sin.

It's time to step out and stay out. Ask God to help you roll a stone over the opening. Allow the Spirit to renew your mind and help you live a pure life for Him.

---

*What sin still calls to you from the tomb?*
*What stone can God help you roll*
*in front of the opening?*

# BE THE MAN WHO AVOIDS RIVALRIES

*In your relationships with one another, have the same mindset as Christ Jesus: Who, being in very nature God, did not consider equality with God something to be used to his own advantage; rather, he made himself nothing by taking the very nature of a servant, being made in human likeness.*

PHILIPPIANS 2:5–7 NIV

---

The word *rivalry* comes from the Latin *rivus*, which means "brook" and stems from the idea of sharing a brook or stream with a neighbor. The rivalry part comes in when our neighbors across the brook begin to compete with us in terms of status, achievements, or belongings. Haven't we all looked at a neighbor's lawn a bit jealously when it is greener than ours?

But Christians aren't to fall into the trap of rivalry. The only thing in which we should try to outdo each other is kindness. And that only happens when we stop obsessing over our own accomplishments and start focusing on the grace God has given us.

In his letter to the Philippians, Paul wanted church members to rise above rivalries. Using Jesus' relationship with God as the ultimate example, Paul says the Lord "did not consider equality with God something to be used to his own advantage; rather, he made himself nothing by taking the very nature of a servant, being made in human likeness" (Philippians 2:6–7 NIV).

If Jesus, who could have made Himself as glorious on earth as He is in heaven, restrained Himself to become a servant of humanity, we can stop trying to outshine our neighbors. Men of purpose choose neighborly love over neighborhood rivalries.

Instead of looking at our neighbors' lawns, we should be looking for our neighbors' needs. How can we show them God's presence if we're hoping they'll see our new boat? Philippians 2:3 (NIV) says, "Do nothing out of selfish ambition or vain conceit. Rather, in humility value others above yourselves."

---

*Are there any rivalries in your life right now?*
*How can you serve your neighbor today?*

# BE THE MAN WHO VALUES WISDOM

*How much better to get wisdom than gold,*
*to get insight rather than silver!*
PROVERBS 16:16 NIV

On October 23, 2018, an anonymous South Carolina resident became the sole winner of the $1.5 billion jackpot in the Mega Millions lottery. Choosing to stay anonymous, the winner received a one-time cash payment of $877,784,124—the largest jackpot payout to a single winner in United States history.

This resident was represented by self-proclaimed "Lottery Lawyer" Jason Kurland. Kurland has represented multiple lottery winners, advising them how to guard against people who would take advantage of them.

Then, on August 18, 2020, the US Department of Justice announced Kurland and three coconspirators had been indicted in a $107 million scheme to defraud lottery-winning clients. Officials alleged that Kurland took advantage of his clients' trust and good fortune, investing in mob-owned properties and allowing mob connections to pillage his clients' wealth.

Lottery winners may seem lucky to us, but most—not just those who were allegedly bilked by Kurland—end up with regrets. While such wealth may bring worldly goods, it can also devastate relationships, encourage recklessness, and draw the attention of violent people.

Money isn't bad, but people who don't use it wisely can harm both themselves and others. Wisdom prevents harm, which is why Proverbs 16:16 says it is better than gold.

Wise people typically don't play the lottery because they know how likely they are to lose, even if they win. Wisdom is a much better investment! But how can you get it? Just ask!

James 1:5 (NIV) says, "If any of you lacks wisdom, you should ask God, who gives generously to all without finding fault, and it will be given to you."

---

*Have you ever dreamed about winning the lottery? If so, how can you change that dream into a prayer for wisdom?*

# BE THE MAN WHO THINKS ABOUT GOOD THINGS

*Finally, brothers and sisters, whatever is true, whatever is noble, whatever is right, whatever is pure, whatever is lovely, whatever is admirable—if anything is excellent or praiseworthy—think about such things.*
PHILIPPIANS 4:8 NIV

Pathways in the brain are like dirt roads. When we dwell on certain things, we create ruts in the road, making it hard to change course. So the longer we dwell on negative things, the less likely we are to see the positive. But when we focus on the positive, we actually reward our brains with chemicals that reinforce our happiness.

According to an article from Harvard Medical School, an optimistic mindset can help "people cope with disease and recover from surgery. Even more impressive is the impact of a positive outlook on overall health and longevity. Research tells us that an optimistic outlook early in life can predict better health and a lower rate of death during follow-up periods of 15 to 40 years."

These "glass half full" studies are nothing new, however; the Bible has prescribed positive thinking for nearly two thousand years. Philippians 4:8 provides a whole list of things to think about: whatever is true, noble, right, pure, lovely, admirable, excellent, or praiseworthy.

Why? Because our thought process influences our attitudes and actions. Just a few verses earlier, Paul told the Philippians (and all of us) to let go of anxiety and rejoice in all circumstances because this will lead to peace.

"And the peace of God, which transcends all understanding, will guard your hearts and your minds in Christ Jesus" (Philippians 4:7 NIV).

To get started, we need to retrain our brains to dwell on praiseworthy things, to see the world through the lens of God's goodness. Not only will we reap physical benefits, we'll experience the peace of God, which exceeds all understanding.

---

*What do you dwell on the most?*
*How can you retrain your brain*
*to see more of God's goodness?*

# BE THE MAN WHO COUNTS THE COST

*"But don't begin until you count the cost.*
*For who would begin construction of a*
*building without first calculating the cost to*
*see if there is enough money to finish it?"*
LUKE 14:28 NLT

---

There is a photo floating around the internet of a man wearing a T-shirt that reads "Guess who started to make brownies before checking the fridge for eggs?" Have you ever made an emergency run to the grocery store for such a reason?

In Luke's Gospel, Jesus gives two similar illustrations that stress the importance of planning for ultimate success.

"But don't begin until you count the cost. For who would begin construction of a building without first calculating the cost to see if there is enough money to finish it? Otherwise, you might complete only the foundation before running out of money, and then everyone would laugh at you. They would say, 'There's the person who started that building and couldn't afford to finish it!' Or what king would go to war against another king without first sitting down with his counselors to discuss whether his army of 10,000 could defeat the 20,000 soldiers marching against him? And if he can't, he will send a delegation to discuss terms of peace while the enemy is still far away" (Luke 14:28–32 NLT).

The point of Jesus' illustrations isn't a literal warning against hastily building a tower or starting a war. It is to warn against halfhearted efforts to follow Christ. Jesus drives His point home in verse 33 (NLT): "So you cannot become my disciple without giving up everything you own."

The cost of following Jesus isn't just expensive; it is exclusive. Men of purpose are willing to pay the price of discipleship because they know following Jesus is, despite the cost, the best deal in history.

---

*Are you willing to pay the price daily to follow Christ? How can you pray against a halfhearted commitment to Jesus?*

# BE THE MAN WHO LIVES SACRIFICIALLY

*Greater love hath no man than this,*
*that a man lay down his life for his friends.*
JOHN 15:13 KJV

---

Animal altruism—the tendency for animals to sacrifice themselves for the good of their offspring or group—has always been a thorn in the side of Darwinism. As a real but puzzling natural phenomenon, altruism has been the subject of many scientific theories.

The spider *Stegodyphus lineatus*, after delivering a small clutch of young, feeds them with regurgitated food. After a couple weeks, when the little spiders are strong enough, they kill and consume her, leaving an empty exoskeleton behind. Throughout the process, the mother spider does nothing to protect herself from her fate. Talk about a mother's love!

While it is instinctual for some animals to sacrifice for their offspring, humanity's strongest instinct is self-preservation. Yes, people are often willing to die for their own kids, but what about for friends?

What about for strangers? What about for enemies?

Jesus says in John 15:13 (KJV), "Greater love hath no man than this, that a man lay down his life for his friends."

Romans 5:8 (KJV) says, "But God commendeth his love toward us, in that, while we were yet sinners, Christ died for us."

Whether we are friends of Jesus or enemies of God, Christ laid down His life for us. Like the altruistic spider, Jesus died to give us life. So what are we to do with that information? Jesus tells us in John 15:12 (KJV): "This is my commandment, That ye love one another, as I have loved you."

We should sacrifice our desires, our preferences, and our lives to share Christ's love with others. Self-preservation has no place here. Men of purpose look for opportunities to lay down everything for Christ's sake.

---

*Have you ever been the recipient of someone else's sacrifice? What desires could you renounce to show love to someone else?*

# BE THE MAN WHO DOESN'T ABUSE HIS AUTHORITY

*But Jesus called them together and said,
"You know that the rulers in this world lord it over
their people, and officials flaunt their authority
over those under them. But among you it will be
different. Whoever wants to be a leader among you
must be your servant, and whoever wants to be
first among you must become your slave."*
MATTHEW 20:25–27 NLT

Power does strange things to people. Studies show that, while people in power are more likely to see the big picture, they are also more likely to engage in risky behavior.

Another study showed a correlation between power and rude behavior. While the connection may seem obvious to some, science has confirmed that drivers of high-end vehicles are likely to cut off other drivers 30 percent of the time, compared to drivers of lower-end vehicles at 7 percent of the time.

These problems may stem from how authority

affects the brain. MRI scans reveal that motor resonance—a brain function responsible for allowing us to see things from other perspectives—is lower in powerful people than in the powerless. Whatever the reason, however, people in power shouldn't be excused for acting like jerks.

As the ultimate authority, Jesus knows how humans behave when given a taste of power. That's why He specifically instructed His followers to serve one another. Men of purpose, whether they possess authority or not, must strive for empathy.

Jesus is our perfect example. He spoke the world into being then took on human form to save us. The world is His footstool, but He bent down and washed His disciples' filthy feet. He could have claimed His rightful throne in heaven at any time, but He chose a crown of thorns and a sinner's cross instead.

Matthew 20:28 (NLT) says, "For even the Son of Man came not to be served but to serve others and to give his life as a ransom for many."

When we find ourselves in power, we cannot allow it to blind us to the perspectives of others. We must be leaders who serve, because we are servants of the ultimate authority.

---

*Have you ever been affected by power?*
*How can you mix empathy with authority?*

# BE THE MAN WHO TAKES RESPONSIBILITY FOR HIS ACTIONS

*Do not be deceived: God cannot be mocked. A man reaps what he sows. Whoever sows to please their flesh, from the flesh will reap destruction; whoever sows to please the Spirit, from the Spirit will reap eternal life.*
GALATIANS 6:7–8 NIV

Actions have consequences. It's a fundamental rule of life, but in our broken world, it isn't always fairly applied. Speeding doesn't always result in a ticket, and innocent people are sometimes convicted of a crime.

Similarly, good deeds often go unrewarded. Our efforts at home are frequently ignored, and our safe driving doesn't mean a thing when someone rear-ends us.

While justice may be subjective here on earth, it won't be forever. We serve an eternal God who is perfectly just, so our present actions will be rewarded eventually.

Galatians 6:7–8 (NIV) says, "Do not be deceived: God cannot be mocked. A man reaps what he sows. Whoever sows to please their flesh, from the flesh will reap destruction; whoever sows to please the Spirit, from the Spirit will reap eternal life."

We can't control the actions of others, but we can take responsibility for our own. As men of purpose, we must admit when we've acted selfishly or wronged someone.

We must also accept our responsibility to do good. As bearers of God's image and adopted heirs of His kingdom, we are called to a higher level of accountability. Fortunately, He'll never give us more than we can handle.

"No temptation has overtaken you except what is common to mankind. And God is faithful; he will not let you be tempted beyond what you can bear. But when you are tempted, he will also provide a way out so that you can endure it" (1 Corinthians 10:13 NIV).

Whether the world demands it or not, it's time to take responsibility for our actions. By doing so, we embrace God's love of justice and rely on His strength to help us succeed.

---

*Do you take responsibility for your actions? Do you accept the responsibility that comes with being a Christian?*

# BE THE MAN WHO LAUGHS WELL

*Obscene stories, foolish talk, and coarse jokes—these are not for you. Instead, let there be thankfulness to God.*
EPHESIANS 5:4 NLT

Two hunters are out in the woods when one of them collapses. He's not breathing, and his eyes are glazed . . .so his friend calls 911. "My buddy is dead!" he gasps. "What should I do?" The operator replies, "Calm down, sir. I can help. First make sure that he's dead." There's a silence, then a loud bang. Back on the phone, the hunter says, "Okay, now what?"

According to British researcher Richard Wiseman, this is scientifically proven to be the funniest joke in the world. (Science actually has a lot to say about humor.)

Doctors at the Mayo Clinic say laughter has a number of physical and emotional benefits. And many studies have shown that funny men are more attractive to women. The ability to be funny is sociologically linked to masculinity.

"If we're not good at being funny—like if we're not tall or not making money—we might feel a masculinity threat where we don't feel like we're living up to our own internal standards of what we should be as men," says Thomas Ford, a psychology professor at Western Carolina University. When this threat to masculinity is felt, some guys respond by shifting their humor toward sexist jokes and rude stories (what Ephesians 5:4 refers to as "obscene stories, foolish talk, and coarse jokes"). These may boost the teller's feeling of masculinity, even while ruining their chances of attracting a mate.

The kind of humor we use matters, not only to women, but to God. The way to be attractive to both? Stay positive. Dwell on things to be thankful for and offer prayers of gratitude to God. By getting the focus off yourself, you won't feel the threats to your masculinity, which will actually enhance your attractiveness. Funny, right?

---

*What does your sense of humor say about your relationship to God? How can thankfulness help you shift your perspective?*

# BE THE MAN WHO
# STAYS SHARP

*As iron sharpens iron,
so a friend sharpens a friend.*
PROVERBS 27:17 NLT

---

Weren't friendships easier as kids? It seemed like anyone could be friends on the playground. Friendships naturally formed around commonalities. If you watched the same television shows or liked the same sports or read the same books, you were friends.

Friendships don't come as easily for adults. Married guys with kids or full-time jobs—or both—have limited amounts of time to hang out with their buddies. Older guys whose kids have left the house have the time but maybe not the willpower, having fallen out of the practice of making friends long ago.

Yet, the Bible says friendship is important because it keeps us sharp. As one iron blade is used to hone another, so too can friends help us fulfill our intended purpose. This doesn't mean we sit around sharing our feelings all the time. It means sharing a common mission to follow Christ, glorify God, and live by the power of the Spirit. Our enemy wants us to think we're alone against the world, but our friends remind us we're in it together.

Not only do we share a mission, we share information. Friends talk about life! In John 15:15 (NLT), Jesus clarified His relationship with His disciples, saying, "I no longer call you slaves, because a master doesn't confide in his slaves. Now you are my friends, since I have told you everything the Father told me."

So how do you make friends? Find some guys who share your interests and values and spend time with them. Church is a great place to start!

---

*What interests do you have that could be the basis for a friendship? How can you push yourself to make new friends?*

# BE THE MAN WHO IS COURTEOUS

*They must not slander anyone and must avoid quarreling. Instead, they should be gentle and show true humility to everyone.*
TITUS 3:2 NLT

Courtesy isn't commonly associated with manliness. The stereotypical man belches loudly then mutters, "Excuse me," but only in the presence of a female. He works hard, fights hard, and doesn't take guff from anyone. Courteous behavior—manners, gentle speech, genuine interest in others, a humble attitude, and so on—is considered old-fashioned. But it shouldn't be.

Christians are called to a higher, more difficult standard. Bodily functions come naturally, and while holding them in may not always be possible, we shouldn't glory in their expulsion. Rudeness doesn't help in drawing people to Christ. Respecting others with everything that comes out of us, burps included, will better allow them to see God's love in us since they won't be closing their eyes and shaking their heads.

While common courtesy is one aspect of our call as Christians, real courtesy begins in the heart and reveals itself in our attitude. Just like body functions, masculine pride comes naturally. Pride is born out of a selfish heart, while humility puts others before itself.

Humility doesn't try to convince the world we are weak. It restrains our strength like we are a muscle car driving slowly through a school zone. Sure, we could press the pedal to the metal and show those school kids what speed really means, but we should be more concerned with keeping them safe.

Philippians 2:3–4 (NLT) reminds us, "Don't be selfish; don't try to impress others. Be humble, thinking of others as better than yourselves. Don't look out only for your own interests, but take an interest in others, too."

It's time for men to accept the challenge of being courteous again. Are you in?

---

*Do you struggle with rudeness?*
*How might you convert pride into humility?*

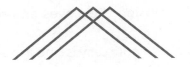

# BE THE MAN WHO
# UNDERSTANDS CONSENT

*"For this reason a man will leave his father and mother and be united to his wife, and the two will become one flesh." This is a profound mystery— but I am talking about Christ and the church.*

Ephesians 5:31–32 NIV

Sex is incredible. God made it so people could experience pleasure—physically, emotionally, and spiritually—as they join with Him in the act of creating new life. While Satan has twisted the goodness of sex to exclude the spiritual element, physical and emotional relationships cannot healthily exist without it. Paul recognized this in Ephesians 5:31–32 when he compared the physical aspect of a marriage to Christ's relationship to the church.

Every physical and emotional relationship should operate with spiritual sensitivity. It may be strange to consider, but every kiss and handhold, every caress and sexual act has spiritual ramifications. This is obviously true with relationships outside of marriage.

But even within a marriage, our sexual relationship won't reflect Christ's relationship with the church if it is marked by selfishness instead of joyful admiration and consensual enjoyment.

There's a reason God offers salvation as a gift instead of a command. He wants us to want Him, but He allows us to make that choice. In romantic relationships, consent is just as important. We want to be wanted, treating affection as a gift, not a command.

Consent isn't only important for choosing to be sexually active; it is important in choosing not to be. First Corinthians 7:5 (NIV) says, "Do not deprive each other except perhaps by mutual consent and for a time, so that you may devote yourselves to prayer. Then come together again so that Satan will not tempt you because of your lack of self-control."

When our relationship with God is pure, our relationships with others will be pure as well.

---

*Is your sexual relationship a reflection of Christ and the church or an outlet for selfishness? How do you view consent in relationships?*

# BE THE MAN WHO GUARDS HIS TONGUE

*If you claim to be religious but don't control
your tongue, you are fooling yourself,
and your religion is worthless.*
JAMES 1:26 NLT

When you squeeze a tube of toothpaste, toothpaste comes out. If you squeeze out too much, too bad. It's not going back in.

When life squeezes you—when you hit your thumb with a hammer, when you get cut off in traffic, when your boss tells you to dust off your résumé because your position is gone—what's inside is what comes out. Jesus said in Luke 6:45 (NLT), "A good person produces good things from the treasury of a good heart, and an evil person produces evil things from the treasury of an evil heart. What you say flows from what is in your heart."

Like toothpaste, words that spurt from your mouth are never going back in.

Being a man of purpose means both guarding your

tongue and filling your mind with good things so the words that do escape aren't bad.

If you want good things to flow from the treasury of your heart, you need to make sure your treasury is well stocked. For this, Paul's prayer for the Ephesian church applies to you too: "May you experience the love of Christ, though it is too great to understand fully. Then you will be made complete with all the fullness of life and power that comes from God" (Ephesians 3:19 NLT).

The last similarity between using toothpaste and guarding your tongue is that both should be part of a regular routine. Just like a cavity-filled mouth uses toothpaste only before a visit to the dentist, a sin-filled life asks to be filled with God's power only before going to church.

---

*What words come out when life squeezes you? How often do you pray to be filled with God's goodness?*

# BE THE MAN WHO
# IS WATCHFUL

*Be sober, be vigilant; because your*
*adversary the devil, as a roaring lion,*
*walketh about, seeking whom he may devour.*
1 PETER 5:8 KJV

As a missionary and explorer, Dr. David Livingstone brought his faith to Africa, opening the continent for other missionaries and shining a light on the inhumane practice of slavery. For his efforts, Livingstone has been commemorated with statues and town names across the globe, but there is one particularly famous honor that he strongly disliked—an artistic portrayal of his being attacked by a lion.

Livingstone was asked for help by a village overrun by lions. He shot one of the beasts and, thinking it was mortally wounded, approached to finish it off. But the lion still had fight in it, and Livingstone's arm was mauled before the creature was slain.

The apostle Peter described the devil as a roaring lion, seeking whom he may devour. But our adversary is also a sly lion, lying in wait for an unwary victim to get too close. Sin doesn't always roar. It often purrs, begging us to scratch its belly before unsheathing its claws.

We as men of purpose are wary of the devil's schemes. We know which areas hold temptations, and we are watchful in new situations that might hold hidden temptations. In both instances, we pray as we watch.

Ephesians 6:18 (NIV) says, "And pray in the Spirit on all occasions with all kinds of prayers and requests. With this in mind, be alert and always keep on praying for all the Lord's people."

It isn't by our own efforts that we guard against sin; it is when we watch with the Spirit and are empowered by the Lord to stand against temptation. That's when the king of this world's jungle will flee before the King of Kings.

---

*Have you ever been lulled into thinking the devil is dead? How can you be watchful against sin in your life?*

# BE THE MAN WHO IS
# GENEROUS TO OTHERS

*Yes, you will be enriched in every way so that you
can always be generous. And when we take your
gifts to those who need them, they will thank God.*
2 CORINTHIANS 9:11 NLT

In a 2017 study, researchers from the University of
Zurich in Switzerland studied the link between generosity and happiness. Participants were promised one
hundred dollars over the course of a few weeks. Half
of the participants were asked to think about spending
the money on themselves. The other half were asked
how they would use the money for someone else. In
the following weeks, those who were generous reported having lower stress levels and higher degrees
of happiness than those who were selfish.

God loves generosity. As the Giver of all good
gifts, He is the embodiment of generosity. And when
He gives generously to you, He isn't doing it so you'll
keep His gifts to yourself. He's doing it so you can be
generous like Him.

In Luke 6:38 (NLT), Jesus says, "Give, and you will receive. Your gift will return to you in full—pressed down, shaken together to make room for more, running over, and poured into your lap. The amount you give will determine the amount you get back."

And in Acts 20:35 (NLT), Paul says, "I have been a constant example of how you can help those in need by working hard. You should remember the words of the Lord Jesus: 'It is more blessed to give than to receive.'"

God designed us to be happier when we are generous, but our sin nature encourages us to be selfish. Being a man of purpose means looking beyond our wants and using our blessings to bless others. When we do, we get the benefit of happiness, knowing that God is being glorified through our actions.

---

*How have you been blessed in a way you can share with others? How can you thank God for others' generosity to you?*

# BE THE MAN WHO
# LETS GO OF ANGER

*"In your anger do not sin": Do not let the
sun go down while you are still angry,
and do not give the devil a foothold.*
Ephesians 4:26–27 niv

---

Anger happens. In itself, anger isn't bad. Some things are worth getting angry about: sin, injustice, the perversion of goodness. But these are rarely the anger-causing issues men deal with.

Most of us get angry when we perceive a threat to ourselves or our comfort. A person sits in your favorite chair. Someone has taken food that clearly had your name on it from the work fridge. The guy in front of you is going ten miles under the speed limit, but you're in a no-passing zone. If just reading any of those things gets your blood boiling, you have some work to do.

Anger is a natural response to stress or frustration. As such, you can use it to identify areas in your life that need God's attention. Feel the anger. Don't stifle it or ignore it. Allow it to guide you in prayer.

Do people get on your nerves? Pray for them, leaving them in God's capable hands. Pray you'll learn to love and accept them despite the annoying things they do. Thank God for bringing this person into your life so you can practice the patience He has shown to you.

Ignoring anger or allowing it to fester only hardens it into resentment. If the devil can get you to focus on yourself, how you've been wronged and what kind of treatment you deserve, he's successfully distracted you from seeing the needs of others and from praising God for His goodness.

Is it hard to be angry without sinning? Of course! But you can do all things through Him who gives you strength (see Philippians 4:13).

---

*What things make you angry? How can those things guide your prayers?*

# BE THE MAN WHO IS CREATED IN GOD'S IMAGE

*So God created man in his own image,*
*in the image of God created he him;*
*male and female created he them.*
GENESIS 1:27 KJV

---

Have you ever seen a photo of your dad or grandpa when they were the age you are now? Sometimes, we look like them or sound like them or act like them. We bear their image because they helped make us. When others see you, they see the evidence of your ancestors.

The whole human race was created in the image of God. Some people think this means we physically resemble God (or, more accurately, Jesus, the second Person of the Trinity). Some think we have God's capacity for morality and ethics in ways animals don't. The main point of bearing God's image is not *how* we resemble Him; the point is that we *do*.

Since we reflect God's image, our treatment of each other becomes a reflection of how we treat Him.

That's why murder is such a big deal in God's book. Genesis 9:6 (NIV) says, "Whoever sheds human blood, by humans shall their blood be shed; for in the image of God has God made mankind."

We should always remember we were made in God's image, not the other way around. Anne Lamott wrote in her book *Bird by Bird*, "You can safely assume you've created God in your own image when it turns out that God hates all the same people you do."

Being a man of purpose means not only recognizing God's image when you look in the mirror, but seeing Him in every face you meet. It means loving others simply because they bear God's image too. It means using your hands for His work, your mind for His thoughts, and your gifts for His glory.

---

*Do you see others as God's image bearers?*
*How can you help people see God's image in you?*

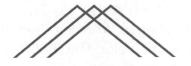

# BE THE MAN WHO IS CREATIVE IN GOD'S IMAGE

*In the beginning God created*
*the heaven and the earth.*
GENESIS 1:1 KJV

The first thing the Bible teaches us about God is how creative He is. He created light, darkness, land, water, plants, animals, and finally us. No two things are alike.

Psalm 104:24 (NLT) says, "O LORD, what a variety of things you have made! In wisdom you have made them all. The earth is full of your creatures."

Consider beetles, a mere subgroup of insects in the animal kingdom. As of now, more than 350,000 different species of beetles have been discovered, and there may be even more.

God must like beetles! But only humans are made in His image, sharing some of His attributes and abilities. We convert our thoughts into art, music, and literature. We build skyscrapers, furniture, and fantastic meals with our hands. We invent and create, not exactly like God did in the beginning, but from the resources He has provided.

Although He has given us the tools for the job, we sometimes hesitate to be creative. Usually, it's because we are afraid our creation will merit rebuke instead of praise, or attention when we prefer not to be seen. But by neglecting this aspect of our identity, we miss out on part of God's goodness.

Creativity doesn't have to be seen or praised to be worthwhile. Even the simplest act of creation teaches us how difficult, as well as how rewarding, it can be.

So draw a picture. Write a story. Build a chair. Create something that didn't exist before, and discover the joy God had in making you.

---

*Do you consider yourself creative?*
*How will you express your creativity?*

# BE THE MAN WHO DOESN'T FEAR TRANSITIONS

*"Be strong and courageous. Do not be afraid or
terrified because of them, for the Lord your God goes
with you; he will never leave you nor forsake you."*
Deuteronomy 31:6 niv

---

Moses was eighty years old when he encountered God
in the burning bush. Living peacefully as a shepherd,
he may have thought his days in Egypt were long
behind him. Then came the plagues, the miracles, the
pillar of fire, the commandments, and, for forty long
years, the wilderness.

Forty years is a long time to follow someone.
Whole generations of Israelites grew up in the wilderness, having never experienced their nation's captivity
in Egypt. But the time had come for a change in leadership. At age 120, Moses knew it was time for Joshua
to lead the nation of Israel into the Promised Land.

Not only were the Israelites preparing to fight
enemies in a foreign land, they were now facing a
change in leadership—a transition just as daunting

as the upcoming battles. However, Moses' advice to both Joshua and the Israelites was the same: "Be strong and courageous" (see Deuteronomy 31:6–7).

Moses wasn't telling them to simply "not fear" the upcoming changes; rather, he gave them a reason for courage: "For the LORD your God goes with you; he will never leave you nor forsake you."

No matter what transitions are taking place in your life, there is one thing that never changes: God is with you. He walks beside you in times of peace and fights on your behalf in times of trouble. Whether you are tackling new responsibilities, exploring a new relationship, or starting a new chapter of your life, God is there.

Our strength and courage are not in ourselves. They are in the Lord our God.

---

*What transitions can you place
into God's hands? How can
you combat fear with trust?*

# BE THE MAN WHO DOESN'T TRY TO IMPRESS PEOPLE

*Obviously, I'm not trying to win the approval of people, but of God. If pleasing people were my goal, I would not be Christ's servant.*
GALATIANS 1:10 NLT

---

When it was initially published in 1936, Dale Carnegie's book *How to Win Friends and Influence People* was an instant success, requiring seventeen printings in its first year alone. The book's popularity has continued, and many consider it to be one of the most influential books of all time.

Carnegie's advice has been used by businesses to train leaders and improve employee communications. It's helped businessmen like Warren Buffett gain wealth, but it's also helped cult leaders like Charles Manson convince their followers to kill. While Carnegie's book contains many exemplary guidelines—be a good listener, give honest and sincere appreciation—some can be used for manipulation. In other words, the method may be good while the focus is all wrong.

Our goal in life should not be getting people to like us or convincing them to do what we want. Our goal should be pleasing God.

Paul said as much in Galatians 1:10 (NLT): "Obviously, I'm not trying to win the approval of people, but of God. If pleasing people were my goal, I would not be Christ's servant."

The apostle John lamented those who recognized the Messiah privately but not in front of the human religious authorities of the day. He said, "For they loved the praise of men more than the praise of God" (John 12:43 KJV).

Pleasing people can be an addictive habit, giving us instant gratification in the form of smiles, thanks, and attaboys. When this becomes our focus, our actions— no matter how good they are—become expressions of selfishness, far removed from our ultimate goal of giving praise to God.

---

*Have you ever been guilty of trying to please people rather than God? How might you remove the focus from yourself in order to better influence people for God?*

# BE THE MAN WHO HAS SELF-CONTROL

*If you find honey, eat just enough—*
*too much of it, and you will vomit.*
PROVERBS 25:16 NIV

---

Honey is pretty amazing. Here are a few fun facts about it:

- Made from plant nectar by bees, honey has antibacterial and antifungal properties and has been used as a medicine for thousands of years.
- Bees produce honey as a winter food source, but since they make two to three times as much as they need, humans reap the benefits.
- In its lifetime, a worker bee will only make one-twelfth of a teaspoon of honey.
- Honeybees share information on food sources with each other by performing a "waggle dance."

As amazing as it is, too much honey can be pretty awful. Think of the bees who spent their whole lives making a twelfth of a teaspoon of honey just for you to throw it up because you ate too much. They'd do a waggle dance of shame right in your face.

Of course, Proverbs 25:16 isn't talking only about honey. Too much of anything can lead to trouble. Too many doughnuts will add doughiness to your frame. Too much reading or screen time will steal time away from family and important projects. In each instance, self-control is vital.

Some people see self-control as refraining from doing bad things, but it applies to good things too. If self-control doesn't come naturally to you, don't worry. It's a supernatural gift of the Holy Spirit (see Galatians 5:22–23). All we need to do is ask for God's help.

---

*When you indulge in something, are you tempted to overindulge? How will you pray for self-control in every situation?*

# BE THE MAN WHO GOES TO CHURCH

*Let us think of ways to motivate one another
to acts of love and good works. And let us not
neglect our meeting together, as some people do,
but encourage one another, especially now that
the day of his return is drawing near.*
HEBREWS 10:24–25 NLT

According to research by Gallup, church membership has been on the decline for years. On average, 69 percent of US adults were members of a church in 1998–2000, compared with 52 percent in 2016–2018. During the same time frame, people who claimed to have no religious affiliation at all rose from 8 to 19 percent.

Times have changed. As people become more technologically connected on a global scale, actual in-person relationships are suffering. Churches, along with other institutions, are losing the confidence of younger generations.

Pessimists may be tempted to give up. What is

the point of church membership when we can watch sermons online, give charitably over our smartphones, and stay up to date on social media?

If church were nothing more than soaking up religious instruction, there wouldn't be a point in meeting together. Church attendance is not about becoming better sponges; it's about applying truths, cleaning up our lives and communities, and learning how to better allow the Holy Spirit to work in and through us.

There are crucial differences between interacting in-person and interacting with someone's social media persona. Most people are unlikely to reveal negative things about themselves online, so we rarely know how to encourage them. By spending time with real people, we get to know their real struggles.

As Hebrews 10:25 says, the day of Christ's return is drawing near. We can't afford to ignore our responsibilities as the body of Christ by neglecting each other's needs. It's time for us to step up and reach out for in-person encouragement, instruction, and engagement with the Holy Spirit.

---

*Do you regularly attend church? How could you be less of a sponge and more of a cleaner?*

# BE THE MAN WHO HAS PEACE

*"Peace I leave with you; my peace I give you.
I do not give to you as the world gives. Do not
let your hearts be troubled and do not be afraid."*
JOHN 14:27 NIV

This world has a lot to offer. God made it with beautiful sunrises, nourishing fruits and vegetables, and awe-inspiring thunderstorms. But when sin entered the world, things began breaking down. The sun still rises, but now it shines on war-torn lands. The earth still grows food, but the greedy hoard it up while others go hungry. Thunderstorms are still amazing, but they can and do sometimes kill.

The world holds many wonders, but lasting peace isn't one of them. The peace of this world is like the eye of a hurricane—a brief lull in the middle of destruction. Real peace is available, but it's not from this earth.

Jesus said in John 14:27 (NIV), "Peace I leave with you; my peace I give you. I do not give to you as the world gives. Do not let your hearts be troubled and do not be afraid."

Our peace—a supernatural peace that doesn't depend on our circumstances—comes from Jesus. Bad days, pain, and earthly sorrows can never take away the peace Jesus gives.

Jesus' peace is found when God Almighty accepts us—despite our sins—into His family. He finds us faultless, seeking no payment beyond the one Jesus made on the cross. Jesus' peace is not simply the absence of punishment; it is rooted in His all-surpassing love, which this world cannot take away.

When we as Christ's followers live in this peace, sinners will see our calm and know its source is supernatural. We are to spread Jesus' peace as we spread His Gospel, knowing we can't have one without the other.

---

*Are you a living example of Jesus' peace?*
*How can you shift your focus*
*to be calm in a crisis?*

# BE THE MAN WHO DOESN'T LET HIS PAST DICTATE HIS FUTURE

*No, dear brothers and sisters, I have not achieved it,
but I focus on this one thing: Forgetting the past and
looking forward to what lies ahead, I press on to reach
the end of the race and receive the heavenly prize for
which God, through Christ Jesus, is calling us.*
PHILIPPIANS 3:13–14 NLT

As a religious teacher, Jesus called some unlikely disciples. A bunch of them were fishermen, not known to be the best or brightest of their day, and one was a tax collector—basically a Jewish traitor who collected money for the Roman empire. Then there was Paul, a bloodthirsty Pharisee bent on snuffing out Christianity. Nothing about these men's questionable pasts qualified them for the honor of learning at the Son of God's feet or imparting God's wisdom to others.

Moses was raised by the oppressors of the Israelite nation and fled after committing murder. David was a murderer *and* an adulterer. Joseph was a tattletale whose brothers hated him for his pride.

The Bible overflows with stories of men whose pasts were redeemed by God for His glory. The same can be true for you.

Have you lived a sinful life? Sure. Who hasn't? Are you worried you're too old to change? Those worries are unfounded.

Jesus' sacrifice has set us free from the sins of our past. He has set us apart for God's use. But when we keep fixating on our past, we can never move toward God's future for us.

If Paul had dwelled on his former misdeeds, we wouldn't have half of the New Testament. If Moses had let his fear stop him from calling on Pharaoh, he wouldn't have led the Israelites out of Egypt. If you let your past sins stop you from obeying God's call, you'll miss out on seeing Him act in and through you.

---

*Does your past get in the way of following God? How can you thank Him for rescuing you and move on in grace?*

# BE THE MAN WHO KNOWS WHERE SUCCESS COMES FROM

*Uzziah sought God during the days of Zechariah, who taught him to fear God. And as long as the king sought guidance from the LORD, God gave him success.*
2 CHRONICLES 26:5 NLT

---

Success is often associated with trailblazers who find wealth, power, or the mastery of some ability. We hear the rags-to-riches story of some leader and think, "They've sure made a success of themselves," or we assign success to a star athlete on account of their winning.

The man of purpose, however, forgoes such a definition, seeing it as rooted in selfishness. True success is found in the original meaning of the word *succeed*, which is "to follow after." At its root, success is simply the accomplishment of a desired end.

We need to think of success not in terms of trailblazing but in terms of following. We can only be successful if we follow the trail marks and arrive at the proper destination. This can be a big mental shift for those of us who think asking for directions is an admission of failure.

Second Chronicles tells the story of Uzziah, the boy-king of Judah who had military success when he sought guidance from the Lord. "Uzziah provided the entire army with shields, spears, helmets, coats of mail, bows, and sling stones. And he built structures on the walls of Jerusalem, designed by experts to protect those who shot arrows and hurled large stones from the towers and the corners of the wall. His fame spread far and wide, for the LORD gave him marvelous help, and he became very powerful" (2 Chronicles 26:14–15 NLT).

But that power led Uzziah into self-reliance, bringing his success to an end (see 2 Chronicles 26:16). If we want success, we must seek God's guidance and run from self-reliance.

---

*How do you define success?*
*Why does self-reliance lead*
*to failure instead of success?*

# BE THE MAN WHO
# MINDS HIS MONEY

*Dishonest money dwindles away, but whoever
gathers money little by little makes it grow.*
PROVERBS 13:11 NIV

Get-rich-quick schemes are as old as the Garden of
Eden. (What else could you call the serpent's promise
of great reward in exchange for breaking one tiny
rule?) The idea of getting rich with little effort is
incredibly appealing. We can all think of good ways
to use a windfall of cash.

The Nigerian prince email scam is one of the most
infamous get-rich-quick schemes in recent history,
not because of its ability to deceive but because of
how laughably obvious and ill-conceived it is. And
yet, there's a reason we still get those emails from
time to time. The misspelled words and the nonsen-
sical premise of sharing our bank account details to
unlock a dead man's hidden millions are designed so
that only the most foolish would fall for them.

Before we laugh at the ones who take the bait,

however, we should examine how we mind our own money. The reason get-rich-quick schemes work is because they appeal to our desire for instant gratification. If you find yourself living paycheck to paycheck, never putting money into a savings account, you may be your own Nigerian prince.

If you think budgeting lacks spiritual importance, think again. Our approach to money reveals how we value the resources God has entrusted to us. If we spend our whole paycheck on gratifying our selfish desires, we've fallen into the devil's scam. But if we tithe and save little by little, we will be able to give freely whenever the Spirit prompts us.

---

*Do you have a budget? How does your spending reflect your spiritual values?*

# BE THE MAN WHO DOESN'T PROCRASTINATE

*"You also must be ready all the time, for the Son of Man will come when least expected."*
LUKE 12:40 NLT

Deadlines are important. If a book isn't delivered to the publisher on time, for instance, the publisher's production schedule suffers, throwing their budget out of whack. Some authors are better with deadlines than others. Douglas Adams, author of the comic sci-fi classic *The Hitchhiker's Guide to the Galaxy*, once said, "I love deadlines. I love the whooshing noise they make as they go by."

It's one thing to procrastinate when you know a project's due date, but what about when a task has no clear deadline? Jesus told this parable in Luke 12:35–38 (NLT): "Be dressed for service and keep your lamps burning, as though you were waiting for your master to return from the wedding feast. Then you will be ready to open the door and let him in the moment he arrives and knocks. The servants who are ready and waiting for his return will be rewarded. I tell you the truth, he himself will seat them, put on an apron, and serve them as they sit and eat! He may come in the middle of the night or just before dawn. But whenever he comes, he will reward the servants who are ready."

When there is no clear due date, working hard is even *more* important! If we're found faithful, we'll be rewarded. If we aren't faithful, well. . . "The master will return unannounced and unexpected, and he will cut the servant in pieces and banish him with the unfaithful" (Luke 12:46 NLT).

These consequences won't be put off to accommodate our schedule, so we shouldn't put off our responsibilities either. Yes, this includes our work projects, but more importantly, it includes our spiritual responsibility to share the Gospel.

---

*Are you known for missing deadlines?*
*How can you better prioritize*
*your responsibilities?*

# BE THE MAN WHO IS LOYAL

*A friend is always loyal, and a
brother is born to help in time of need.*
PROVERBS 17:17 NLT

The phrase "I've got your back" is probably a recent addition to the English language, dating back to World War II. As soldiers advanced on retreating armies, they used small squads of men to clear out enemy defensive positions. A soldier approaching these strongholds would turn to his buddy and say, "Watch my back," in the hopes that his comrade would defend him against enemies shooting from behind. The request would be answered with, "I've got your back."

Although our enemies remain unseen, we live in a spiritual war zone, and it is vital that we have a loyal squad of men watching our backs. Ephesians 6:12 (NLT) says, "For we are not fighting against flesh-and-blood enemies, but against evil rulers and authorities of the unseen world, against mighty powers in this dark world, and against evil spirits in the heavenly places."

The last thing we want is for one of our friends

to turn us over to the enemy, which is exactly why we should be loyal to our friends. Our loyalty should not be the type that covers up sin or makes excuses for each other. Rather, we should commit first to following God and His commandments. Then we should commit to helping our brothers do likewise.

It isn't when things are going well that our loyalties will be tested, but when everything seems to be falling apart. When our first loyalty is to God, the Holy Spirit empowers us to be better friends and loyal brothers-in-arms. If our loyalty to God starts to crumble, our brothers will hopefully have our back, reminding us who the enemy really is.

---

*Are you loyal to God first?*
*How can you prove your loyalty*
*to your brothers-in-arms?*

# BE THE MAN WHO
# RESPECTS HIS ELDERS

*Thou shalt rise up before the hoary head,*
*and honour the face of the old man,*
*and fear thy God: I am the LORD.*
LEVITICUS 19:32 KJV

---

Old age is hard won but often ill rewarded. With experience and wisdom come aches, pains, and memory loss. Comedian George Burns once quipped, "By the time you're eighty years old you've learned everything. You only have to remember it."

Despite these issues, elderly folks have a lot to offer younger generations. The Bible has a few things to say about respecting and learning from our elders:

- "With the ancient is wisdom; and in length of days understanding" (Job 12:12 KJV).

- "Gray hair is a crown of splendor; it is attained in the way of righteousness" (Proverbs 16:31 NIV).

- "Rebuke not an elder, but intreat him as a

father; and the younger men as brethren"
(1 Timothy 5:1 KJV).

What can we learn? First, our elders could teach us to better value spiritual matters. According to a study by the Pew Research Center, "Religion is a far bigger part of the lives of older adults than younger adults. Two-thirds of adults ages 65 and older say religion is very important to them, compared with just over half of those ages 30 to 49 and just 44 percent of those ages 18 to 29."

What else could we learn? Today's elderly folks lived without how-to videos on YouTube, learning by experience the best ways to build, fix, budget, and plan.

Lastly, many elders are prayer warriors who would love to take your requests before God's throne. The first step in learning from their wisdom is starting a conversation. Honor them by listening and inviting them into our lives. Then, when it is our turn, we can impart their knowledge to the generations that follow us.

---

*When was the last time you had a
conversation with an elderly person?
How could you honor one today?*

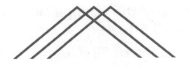

# BE THE MAN WHO DOESN'T GIVE IN TO PEER PRESSURE

*Do not set foot on the path of the wicked or walk in the way of evildoers. Avoid it, do not travel on it; turn from it and go on your way.*
PROVERBS 4:14–15 NIV

---

It's nice to be included. We're wired to crave the safety and acceptance that comes from being part of the crowd. But when the crowd is going the wrong way, safety is the last thing we'll find.

As our culture drifts further from worshipping God and closer to self-deification, things once recognized as sin are becoming celebrated cultural icons. *Wickedness* is no longer a socially acceptable term because of the world's desire to define itself in its own terms.

We can either flow with the world's momentum or stand up for truth as defined in the Bible. Taking a stand won't be easy. We'll surely offend some and make enemies of others, but it is not for us to decide what happens to those who oppose God.

Second Thessalonians 1:6–9 (NIV) says, "God is just:

He will pay back trouble to those who trouble you and give relief to you who are troubled, and to us as well. This will happen when the Lord Jesus is revealed from heaven in blazing fire with his powerful angels. He will punish those who do not know God and do not obey the gospel of our Lord Jesus. They will be punished with everlasting destruction and shut out from the presence of the Lord and from the glory of his might."

When it seems easier to just go along with the world, or when your friends try to convince you sin is no big deal, remember the big picture. Get out of there. Avoid the dangers. Move along toward righteousness.

---

*Why do you think Proverbs 4:14–15 warns against wickedness in multiple ways? Are there any sins you are tempted to label as "no big deal"?*

# BE THE MAN WHO IS EQUIPPED
# FOR EVERY GOOD WORK

*All Scripture is God-breathed and is useful for
teaching, rebuking, correcting and training in
righteousness, so that the servant of God may
be thoroughly equipped for every good work.*
2 TIMOTHY 3:16–17 NIV

There are many screwdrivers in the world: flat head
(slotted), Phillips, Torx (star), Hex, and Robertson
(square), to name a few. Each screwdriver corre-
sponds to a specific screw head design. Try to use a
Phillips screwdriver on a slotted screw, and you'll run
into trouble.

One of the lesser-known screwdrivers is the Birmingham screwdriver. . .which is actually a hammer.
This joke is at the expense of Birmingham, England,
implying its residents solve their problems with brute
force rather than using the right tools.

Psychologist Abraham Maslow made the following
observation in his book *The Psychology of Science*: "I
suppose it is tempting, if the only tool you have is a

hammer, to treat everything as if it were a nail."

How does this relate to our spiritual life? Some men treat the Bible like a Birmingham screwdriver when it's actually a well-stocked toolbox. Second Timothy 3:16–17 (NIV) says, "All Scripture is God-breathed and is useful for teaching, rebuking, correcting and training in righteousness, so that the servant of God may be thoroughly equipped for every good work."

When we need to open our minds, we can turn to James 1:5 (NIV): "If any of you lacks wisdom, you should ask God, who gives generously to all without finding fault, and it will be given to you."

When we need to be corrected, 1 John 1:9 (NIV) offers the solution: "If we confess our sins, he is faithful and just and will forgive us our sins and purify us from all unrighteousness."

Whatever our situation, the Bible has the right tool for the job. But to be better craftsmen, we need to familiarize ourselves with the whole toolbox.

---

*Have you ever treated the Bible like a hammer? What are some verses you can memorize to deal with common issues you face?*

# BE THE MAN WHO
# RESPECTS AUTHORITY

*Everyone must submit to governing authorities.*
*For all authority comes from God, and those in*
*positions of authority have been placed there by God.*
ROMANS 13:1 NLT

---

Americans are born with a confused sense of respect for authority. Our country was founded on rebellion against British rule. Our presidents are chosen by an electoral college that sometimes goes against the majority of voters. It would be easy to say, "I didn't vote for them, so I don't need to respect them." But the easy way is rarely the biblical way.

Romans 13:1 says we must submit to governing authorities because all authority comes from God. This verse was written by Paul, who would eventually be martyred for his faith by Roman authorities. Paul didn't demand respect for these leaders because they were worthy of it in themselves, but rather because they were subject to a greater authority.

Though earthly leaders are not always moral, they

are placed in authority by the One who sees and controls the larger picture for His own purposes. Daniel 2:21 (NLT) says, "He controls the course of world events; he removes kings and sets up other kings. He gives wisdom to the wise and knowledge to the scholars."

The message is echoed in Psalm 75:7 (NLT): "It is God alone who judges; he decides who will rise and who will fall."

So how are we to show respect to authorities who prove themselves unworthy? Through prayer and blessing. When we pray for them, we place them under God's authority instead of ours. And we are to bless them, even when they oppose us and our values. Romans 12:14 (NLT) says, "Bless those who persecute you. Don't curse them; pray that God will bless them."

---

*Do you struggle to respect those in authority? How can you pray for their blessing?*

# BE THE MAN WHO GETS BACK UP

*The godly may trip seven times, but they will get up again. But one disaster is enough to overthrow the wicked.*
PROVERBS 24:16 NLT

---

Being a perfect man of purpose would require you to flawlessly follow God with heart, soul, and strength. But let's be honest—that's impossible for an imperfect man to do. At some point, you'll slip up. Your attention will waver, your focus will shift, and your feet will stumble.

In the Old Testament, there was no prophet like Elijah. Active during Ahab's reign over Israel, Elijah performed many miracles to show God's power. He multiplied food supplies for the widow of Zarephath, and even brought her dead son back to life (see 1 Kings 17:8–24).

Elijah's most famous exploit, however, was his face-off against the prophets of Baal. The challenge took place on Mount Carmel, where each side called upon his own deity to send fire from the heavens. No torches allowed.

After watching Baal's prophets plead fruitlessly for hours, Elijah got bored. First Kings 18:27 (NLT) says, "About noontime Elijah began mocking them. 'You'll have to shout louder,' he scoffed, 'for surely he is a god! Perhaps he is daydreaming, or is relieving himself. Or maybe he is away on a trip, or is asleep and needs to be wakened!' "

After Elijah's turn, God sent a fire that consumed the sacrifice *and* the altar, and the story ends with Baal's prophets being put to the sword. Elijah should have been the epitome of confidence at this point, but immediately following this encounter, he ran and hid from Ahab's wife, Jezebel.

That could have been the end of his story, but it wasn't. Elijah got back up and continued doing God's will until he finally boarded a chariot to heaven, bypassing death entirely. Whenever we fall, Elijah's story should inspire us to get back up and keep moving.

---

*Have you ever slipped up after confidently proclaiming victory for God? What could you accomplish for God by getting back up?*

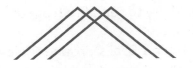

# BE THE MAN WHO LOVES
# WITH WORD AND DEED

*Whoever claims to love God yet hates a brother
or sister is a liar. For whoever does not love their
brother and sister, whom they have seen, cannot
love God, whom they have not seen.*
1 JOHN 4:20 NIV

Words are incredible communication tools. Some
men can do amazing things with grunts and nods, but
words are the best way to convey complex concepts.
And yet, words will always fall short when they are
not accompanied by deeds.

For instance, if a man claims to be a gourmand but
weighs eighty pounds sopping wet, you'd wonder if
he really loves food.

Similarly, when a man says he loves God, there
should be some evidence to support his claim. First
John 4:7–9 (NIV) says, "Dear friends, let us love one
another, for love comes from God. Everyone who
loves has been born of God and knows God. Whoever does not love does not know God, because God

is love. This is how God showed his love among us: He sent his one and only Son into the world that we might live through him."

God authenticated His claim to love us by sending Jesus to rescue us from the penalty of sin. As saved men, we should then pass along God's love to others.

James 2:14–17 (NIV) puts it this way: "What good is it, my brothers and sisters, if someone claims to have faith but has no deeds? Can such faith save them? Suppose a brother or a sister is without clothes and daily food. If one of you says to them, 'Go in peace; keep warm and well fed,' but does nothing about their physical needs, what good is it? In the same way, faith by itself, if it is not accompanied by action, is dead."

If we claim to love God, we must reinforce our words with action. The actions don't save us; they are evidence of our salvation.

---

*Do your words and deeds prove God's love is in you? How can you show someone His love today?*

# BE THE MAN WHO MOVES MOUNTAINS

*"You don't have enough faith," Jesus told them.*
*"I tell you the truth, if you had faith even as small*
*as a mustard seed, you could say to this mountain,*
*'Move from here to there,' and it would move.*
*Nothing would be impossible."*
MATTHEW 17:20 NLT

---

The highest natural point in Florida is Britton Hill, which is located along the top of Florida's panhandle near the Alabama border. Standing at 345 feet above sea level, Britton Hill is the lowest of all fifty states' high points and is dwarfed by some of Miami's skyscrapers.

With a bulldozer, a dump truck, and time, it would not be difficult to add enough dirt to a nearby hill to top Britton Hill's height. Of course, whether this would be officially recognized as the highest natural point (as it would be artificially constructed) is a matter for summit enthusiasts and land surveyors to debate.

When Jesus spoke about moving mountains with our faith, He wasn't talking about Britton Hill. Mount Hermon, one of the highest mountains in Israel, stands at 6,690 feet above sea level. Jesus' Jewish audience would have understood His reference to moving a mountain like Mount Hermon as a way to describe an impossible task.

How much faith, according to Jesus, is needed to do the impossible? Not much. He compared the necessary faith to a mustard seed, 1 to 2 millimeters in size. When we have a little faith in a God who towers over mountains, anything is possible.

Whether the bumps you face in life are the size of Britton Hill, Mount Hermon, or Mount Everest, they become little more than molehills when you fix your eyes on God. As Jeremiah 32:17 (NIV) says: "Ah, Sovereign LORD, you have made the heavens and the earth by your great power and outstretched arm. Nothing is too hard for you."

---

*What mountains do you need God to move for you? How could you shift your focus to Him instead of your mountain?*

## BE THE MAN WHO HAS JOY AMID SUFFERING

*But rejoice, inasmuch as ye are partakers of
Christ's sufferings; that, when his glory shall be
revealed, ye may be glad also with exceeding joy.*
1 Peter 4:13 kjv

---

Joy and suffering aren't typically marketed as a package deal. Joy is usually used to advertise amusement parks, candy, and sugary breakfast cereals. When you imagine joyful moments, things like weddings and birthday parties probably come to mind.

But joy isn't all lollipops and rainbows. Joy is like the finest dark chocolate—bittersweet, rich, and lingering. Best of all—unlike happiness, which is dependent on circumstances—joy is a choice. If it weren't, it would be daft for the Bible to repeatedly command us to rejoice in unhappy circumstances:

- "Consider it pure joy, my brothers and sisters, whenever you face trials of many kinds" (James 1:2 niv).

- "In the midst of a very severe trial, their overflowing joy and their extreme poverty welled up in rich generosity" (2 Corinthians 8:2 NIV).
- "But let all who take refuge in you be glad; let them ever sing for joy. Spread your protection over them, that those who love your name may rejoice in you" (Psalm 5:11 NIV).

How can joy exist in trials, poverty, and persecution? Because joy isn't the absence of suffering but the presence of God. Romans 15:13 (NIV) says, "May the God of hope fill you with all joy and peace as you trust in him, so that you may overflow with hope by the power of the Holy Spirit."

When trials come, we must be intentional about resting in the power of the Holy Spirit. When we do, suffering can reveal the presence of God better than the happiest times. . .and in that presence is joy.

---

*Do you sometimes avoid suffering,*
*thereby avoiding a chance for joy?*
*Would others label you as a joyful person?*

# BE THE MAN WHO DOESN'T JUDGE BY APPEARANCES

*"Stop judging by mere appearances,*
*but instead judge correctly."*
JOHN 7:24 NIV

---

The rule "never judge a book by its cover" is somewhat misleading, originating at a time when all books were similarly bound and thus looked basically identical from the outside. As time progressed and marketing professionals got involved, book covers were designed to appeal to specific buyers. These days, books are practically the *only* things you can judge by their covers.

When it comes to people, however, judging by appearance alone has never been wise. Although our brains are wired to help us form first impressions, we should never presume to know a person's story or abilities based on these impressions.

By appearances alone, Saul, Israel's first king, should have been an amazing leader. He was tall, strong, and good-looking, but his dynasty died with him. God chose David—whose appearance was much less impressive—to be king after Saul.

At David's anointing, even the prophet Samuel questioned whether God had made a mistake. After Samuel suggested one of David's elder brothers might be better suited for kingship, the Lord responded in 1 Samuel 16:7 (NIV): "Do not consider his appearance or his height, for I have rejected him. The LORD does not look at the things people look at. People look at the outward appearance, but the LORD looks at the heart."

As people, we cannot see what's inside a person's heart, nor can we accurately judge a person based on their appearance. How are we to act then? Romans 12:10 (NIV) says, "Be devoted to one another in love. Honor one another above yourselves."

---

*Have you ever had a wrong first impression of someone? How might you better see people through God's eyes?*

# BE THE MAN WHO ACTS AS CHRIST'S AMBASSADOR

*So we are Christ's ambassadors; God is making his appeal through us. We speak for Christ when we plead, "Come back to God!"*
2 CORINTHIANS 5:20 NLT

Ambassadors are the representatives of one country to another. They act as the eyes and ears of their nation, reporting back all they see in the host country. They are also their home country's mouthpiece, advocating for their nation's interests and negotiating on its behalf.

Successful ambassadors are gifted communicators, savvy problem solvers, and experts on both their home and host countries. All embassy employees take the Foreign Service Officers Test and are assigned to a specific track of employment. Some ambassadors are appointed to their posts by heads of state, but most rise through their embassy's ranks, distinguishing themselves by their effort and expertise.

As followers of Christ, we are ambassadors of

God's kingdom. Our citizenship is in heaven and we act as God's agents in a foreign, and sometimes hostile, land. We function as God's eyes and ears, bringing our observations to Him through prayer. We are His mouthpiece to the lost residents of this world, pleading for them to "Come back to God!"

Whether we entered God's service by appointment or choice, we are called to represent God through our actions. We are not representing ourselves; we are on a diplomatic mission for God, and our behavior reflects on His character. If we love as God loves, we perform our duties well; if we hate our neighbors, act selfishly, or show favoritism, we are poor ambassadors for God.

As a man of purpose, it is your job to represent God to the world around you. Get to know Him well, so you can be a good ambassador.

---

*What would you think about a nation whose ambassadors were rude or mean? How can you be a good ambassador for Christ?*

# BE THE MAN WHO
# DRIVES RESPECTFULLY

*The lookout reported, "He has reached them, but he*
*isn't coming back either. The driving is like that of*
*Jehu son of Nimshi—he drives like a maniac."*
2 KINGS 9:20 NIV

---

Jehu—whose reign is outlined in 2 Kings 9–10—was
one of the most intense kings of the Old Testament.
A military commander who was elevated to kingship
by the prophet Elisha's orders, Jehu was a man of
bloodshed, but he was rewarded with a dynasty that
lasted four generations.

As a king, Jehu exacted brutal justice on God's
behalf by putting an end to the wicked leadership of
Ahab and Jezebel; as a man, he was known for another
trait. While other kings are known for their wisdom
or benevolence, Jehu will forever be remembered as
the king who drove like a maniac.

When driving, are you a wild king of the road like
Jehu, your progress marked by roadkill and the cries
of bystanders? Or are you known for your safety

and courtesy? Believe it or not, how you drive is as important to God as everything else you do.

Sometimes we forget this fact, allowing our frustrations to bring out our inner demons. We curse. We shout. We forget other drivers are made in the image of God. And we justify our actions, reactions, and verbal atrocities with the consolation that no one can hear us from our own vehicles.

But God hears. And as a loving parent, God wants better for us. He wants us to drive respectfully. When other drivers get in our way, He wants us to pray a blessing over them. When we are driving on a stretch of highway all alone, He wants us to obey the speed limit, respecting the law of the land and the leaders He's placed in charge.

Whenever you find yourself driving like Jehu, slow down and ask if that's really something you want to be known for.

---

*Are you a different man behind the wheel?*
*How can you honor God with your driving?*

# BE THE MAN WHO HONORS GOD IN EVERYTHING

*Whether therefore ye eat, or drink,*
*or whatsoever ye do, do all to the glory of God.*
1 CORINTHIANS 10:31 KJV

The church of Corinth was divided. Some folks were eating food that had been offered to idols (since idols don't eat much, the food was clearanced out quickly), while others, not wanting their money to support the idol-worshipping industry, were opposed to the practice. Was it better for Christians to be frugal and have more money to help the needy, or was it better to avoid dealing with idol worshippers altogether?

Paul's response was simple. In 1 Corinthians 10:21 (NLT), Paul writes, "You cannot drink from the cup of the Lord and from the cup of demons, too. You cannot eat at the Lord's Table and at the table of demons, too."

An easy answer, right? Well. . .

Paul also writes in 1 Corinthians 10:25–26 (NLT), "So you may eat any meat that is sold in the market place without raising questions of conscience. For 'the earth is the LORD's, and everything in it.' "

This isn't so much a food issue, but a heart issue. If you believe it honors God to save money and use it to provide for His people, buy the meat. If you believe it honors God to avoid idol meat, avoid it. The point is to always honor God in our hearts, regardless of the action.

When our hearts are pointed to God's glory instead of our individual preferences, we won't get caught up in disagreements. We'll do everything—eating, drinking, fixing lawn mowers, washing our hands, blowing our noses, writing books, *everything*—to the glory of God.

---

*How might you shift your focus to give God more glory in your activities? Have you ever fought with other Christians over something trivial?*

# BE THE MAN
# WHO ASKS FIRST

*What causes fights and quarrels among you? Don't
they come from your desires that battle within you?
You desire but do not have, so you kill. You covet but
you cannot get what you want, so you quarrel and
fight. You do not have because you do not ask God.*
JAMES 4:1–2 NIV

In the film *Road to Perdition*, Tom Hanks stars as Mike
Sullivan, a mob enforcer from the 1930s. After his
own family becomes a mob target, Sullivan and his
son, Mike Jr., team up against his former employer
by robbing mob-owned banks.

There is a scene in which Mike Jr. asks his dad
for a cut of the money they're stealing. His dad asks
how much he wants, and the boy quickly replies,
"Two hundred dollars," an astronomical amount for
the time. After a moment of consideration, his dad
agrees to the amount.

After a second of silence, the boy says, "Could I
have had more?"

His father answers, "You'll never know."

Regardless of the circumstances, parents love giving good things to their children. Our Father in heaven is the same way.

In Matthew 7:9–11 (NIV), Jesus says, "Which of you, if your son asks for bread, will give him a stone? Or if he asks for a fish, will give him a snake? If you, then, though you are evil, know how to give good gifts to your children, how much more will your Father in heaven give good gifts to those who ask him!"

God wants to give His children good things, but He wants us to ask for them first. When God blesses us without being asked, we may not notice or feel the same sense of appreciation. When we request and He provides, we can more easily see the relationship between asking and receiving, thereby reinforcing our trust in Him.

God can provide more than we ask. It would be better for us to echo Mike Jr. in saying, "Could I have had more?" instead of never asking at all.

---

*Do you take your requests to God, or do your desires lead you to confrontation with people? How has God already proven His trustworthiness to you?*

# BE THE MAN WHO
# HAS A GOOD HEART

*"A good person produces good things from the treasury of a good heart, and an evil person produces evil things from the treasury of an evil heart. What you say flows from what is in your heart."*
LUKE 6:45 NLT

---

Have you ever heard someone talk about a terrible person and finish by saying, "But they have such a good heart"? You know the speaker either has no idea what they're saying or has a huge blind spot for the person they're describing.

Good-hearted people are kind, thoughtful, and generous. They are not violent against others. They are not cruel to animals. They are not selfish in their attitudes or actions. It isn't difficult to recognize a good-hearted person. Usually, all it takes is a conversation.

Before we label people as good-hearted or evil, however, we need to understand the difference. It is tempting to think we have the power to change our own hearts, but we don't. We are the patients, not the doctor.

Jesus says in Luke 6:43-44 (NLT), "A good tree can't produce bad fruit, and a bad tree can't produce good fruit. A tree is identified by its fruit. Figs are never gathered from thornbushes, and grapes are not picked from bramble bushes."

God is the One who plants, sends the sunshine and rain, and tends His garden with love. We are the trees who bear fruit. Does this mean we have no responsibilities? No. It means our good choices ultimately originate from a perfect and holy God.

None of us have the power to change our own hearts. Only God does. What we *can* do is give our hearts to Him so He can change them for us. Similarly, we can't change the hearts of others. . .but we can introduce them to a God who can.

---

*Can others tell what kind of tree you are by your fruit? Are you letting God control your whole heart to make it all good?*

# BE THE MAN WHO SEES NEEDS AND FILLS THEM

*For we are God's handiwork, created in Christ Jesus to do good works, which God prepared in advance for us to do.*
EPHESIANS 2:10 NIV

---

Which invention revolutionized a key aspect of warfare in the early nineteenth century? If you are thinking about weapons or vehicles, think again. The answer is canned food. Scientist Nicolas Appert developed a method for canning food in glass jars with metal lids, saving armies around the world from rotten rations on the battlefield.

Before long, metal cans replaced glass jars, but opening them required a hammer and chisel. Minor improvements were made over the years, but it wasn't until 1920 that the classic toothed-wheel crank can opener was patented by Charles Arthur Bunker.

Consider for a moment the time gap between the invention of tin cans and the invention of a convenient can opener. Cans around the world were stacking up or being opened in crude ways while much of the food inside went unused.

According to Ephesians 2:10, we are a bit like can openers. We've been designed for a specific purpose. The needs of the world have been stacking up, waiting for us to come along. We ourselves are not the solution. We are simply tools in the hands of God. We cannot nourish any more than a can opener can create food, but we can be the instruments that make nourishment possible.

God has prepared good works specifically for you to do. What needs do you see around you? What cans of blessing will you open for others? What knowledge do you possess that someone else needs?

As a man of purpose, you have been created for God's use. How will you let Him use you today?

---

*What gifts has God given you to use for Him? How can you encourage others to join you in being useful for God?*

# BE THE MAN WHO HAS A GOOD REPUTATION

*A good name is better than precious ointment;*
*and the day of death than the day of one's birth.*
ECCLESIASTES 7:1 KJV

---

What is the value of a reputation? In the Old Order Amish community of Lancaster County, Pennsylvania, reputations have financial ramifications.

In a 2008 interview with NPR's Adam Davidson, Bill O'Brien of Hometown Heritage Bank in Pennsylvania explained how he approaches loans for a community without credit scores. "I'll find out who his dad was," he says. "I'm also interested in who his wife's father is. . . . It takes a team to make a farm go."

Even without credit scores and modern banking tools, Hometown Heritage Bank has done well with vetting its clients by family reputations. "We've never lost any money on an Amish deal," says O'Brien.

Reputations are built over time, and their ramifications transcend finances. Proverbs 22:1 (KJV) says, "A good name is rather to be chosen than great riches, and loving favour rather than silver and gold."

Why is a good name so valuable? Because it helps people see God in us. First Peter 2:12 (NLT) says, "Be careful to live properly among your unbelieving neigh-bors. Then even if they accuse you of doing wrong, they will see your honorable behavior, and they will give honor to God when he judges the world."

Our reputations act as shields against unwarranted accusations, testifying to the life-changing effects of God's presence. For a man of purpose to have a good reputation, his life must show a consistent pattern of God-honoring choices.

Famous basketball coach John Wooden once said, "Be more concerned with your character than your reputation, because your character is what you really are, while your reputation is merely what others think you are."

When we live intentionally for God's glory, we'll have both.

---

*What are you known for?*
*What is your reputation worth?*

# BE THE MAN WHO DOES
# THE FIRST THINGS FIRST

*Put your outdoor work in order and get*
*your fields ready; after that, build your house.*
PROVERBS 24:27 NIV

If you are going to do something, do it right. This doesn't only apply to the level of craftsmanship you apply. It also means completing jobs in the right order, prioritizing some tasks over others, and finishing what you've started.

Being a man of purpose means having a plan. The best plans put each task in the right order. If you're grilling burgers and you want to top them with cheese and bacon, you need to cook some bacon and make sure the cheese is sliced before you fire up the grill. Otherwise, your burgers will get cold, the cheese won't melt properly, and no amount of bacon will rescue the taste.

The wise planner looks at each step of a job and determines its proper order. Which things can be done ahead of time? Which ones simultaneously?

When must I start?

If prioritizing tasks isn't an issue for you, maybe procrastination is. There is a quote, often misattributed to Mark Twain, that says, "If the first thing you do each morning is to eat a live frog, you can go through the day with the satisfaction of knowing that that is probably the worst thing that is going to happen to you all day long."

When eating a live frog is on your to-do list, do it first and move on. Procrastination changes difficult tasks into insurmountable ones.

God wants us to be wise with our time because it's actually His time. Prioritizing tasks and avoiding procrastination allows us to use that time for God's purposes.

---

*How well do you order your to-do list?*
*How often do you procrastinate?*

# BE THE MAN WHO STEPS OUT OF THE BOAT

*Then Peter called to him, "Lord, if it's really you, tell me to come to you, walking on the water." "Yes, come," Jesus said. So Peter went over the side of the boat and walked on the water toward Jesus.*

MATTHEW 14:28–29 NLT

---

Peter was a fisherman before becoming a disciple of Jesus. He knew how water typically works. You can't just traipse across the waves without something holding you up. That's why he and the other disciples had a boat. Boats are great for keeping people afloat.

After a full day of teaching crowds and miraculously feeding them with five loaves of bread and two fish, Jesus needed to recharge. Sending the disciples ahead of Him to the other side of the lake, Jesus went up in the hills to pray. But before the disciples reached the other side, Jesus caught up with them, walking on the water.

It wasn't calm water either. A storm was raging.

Even though several disciples had seafaring backgrounds, they struggled to keep the boat from sinking. They had seen some incredible things, but seeing a figure approaching them on the water after a sleepless night was too much. They thought Jesus was a ghost.

Matthew 14:27 (NLT) says, "But Jesus spoke to them at once. 'Don't be afraid,' he said. 'Take courage. I am here!' "

Peter must have believed it was Jesus, even before calling back to Him. Why else would he offer to test the ghost's identity by stepping onto a stormy lake? Whatever the reason, Peter stepped out. After hours of trying to keep the boat afloat, Peter knew Jesus was an even safer bet for keeping him above water.

When troubles threaten to capsize your boat, look for Jesus. He's not a ghost waiting for you to fail. He's the Savior who will help you find your feet, even on the waves.

---

*What things do you credit with keeping you afloat? Do you have the faith needed to step out of the boat?*

# BE THE MAN WHO LISTENS BEFORE SPEAKING

*To answer before listening—*
*that is folly and shame.*
PROVERBS 18:13 NIV

A baby boy is flexible enough to easily place his foot into his mouth. Some grow up to become men who never learn how to stop, figuratively speaking. Fortunately, there are two surefire ways to prevent yourself from saying something embarrassing. First, you can practice your flexibility and literally put your foot in your mouth so no one can understand what you say. Alternatively, you can listen before speaking.

Listening is the most important part of communication, so how can we improve?

The first step is to focus. Limit anything that would call your attention away from the speaker. Turn off the television. Put down the cell phone. Turn to face the person and maintain eye contact as much as possible.

Second, ask questions based on the information

you're hearing. Ask for clarification. Ask what happened next. Let the speaker know you are following the conversation.

Third—and this is the toughest one for men—listen to understand, not to fix. If the speaker asks for your help or opinion, give it. Otherwise, just listen, showing how much you care about what the speaker is saying.

Lastly, don't interrupt. Nothing will send the message that someone's words are unimportant like cutting that person off. Only when a person is finished talking should you respond.

Listening isn't just a polite thing to do. It will benefit every relationship in your life. And not only human relationships, but your relationship with Christ too! What if the Lord is trying to speak to you, but you've been too distracted to listen?

---

*How would you rate yourself as a listener? Which aspect of listening will you work on today?*

# BE THE MAN WHO GIVES THANKS

*O give thanks unto the L*ORD*; for he is good;*
*for his mercy endureth for ever.*
1 CHRONICLES 16:34 KJV

Imagine giving a gift to a child. The child unwraps it, squeals with delight, and immediately starts using it. The child's parents look at you and say, "Awesome gift! Thanks for giving it to our kid."

What's wrong with this scenario?

The child should have been the one to thank you. The parents might be grateful on their kid's behalf, but they weren't the direct recipients. Even though that's not why you gave the gift, a bit of gratitude on the child's part would have made the gift-giving much more satisfying.

Like joy, gratitude is a choice, not just a feeling. It is the intentional recognition of being the recipient of something good. It would be sad indeed if we were to treat God as the child treated you in the above scenario.

What are some simple things to be thankful for? Life, breath, food, water, God's mercy, the freedom to make your own choices. These are all worthy of your gratitude, but if you want to go even further, try being thankful for hard things as well.

First Thessalonians 5:18 (NLT) says, "Be thankful in all circumstances, for this is God's will for you who belong to Christ Jesus."

When a relationship breaks down, thank God for never forsaking you. When you lose your income, thank God for His miraculous provision. When others reject you or mock you for your faith, thank God you can experience what Christ suffered on earth.

Gratefulness is a muscle that's strengthened through intentional use. Are you working it out daily?

---

*What is a good thing you are thankful for? What is a hard thing you can be thankful for?*

# BE THE MAN WHO NUMBERS HIS DAYS

*So teach us to number our days,*
*that we may apply our hearts unto wisdom.*
PSALM 90:12 KJV

---

With a couple of notable exceptions (see Genesis 5:23–24 and 2 Kings 2:11), everyone dies. Our days are numbered, whether we realize it or not. Psalm 90 opens with the stark difference between God's infinite glory and man's brief life span: "A thousand years in your sight are like a day that has just gone by, or like a watch in the night. Yet you sweep people away in the sleep of death—they are like the new grass of the morning: In the morning it springs up new, but by evening it is dry and withered" (Psalm 90:4–6 NIV).

While a bit morbid, the Latin phrase *memento mori*—which means "Remember you will die"—is actually a reminder to live. If death were not a concern, we wouldn't worry about how we spend our time any more than a billionaire worries about clipping coupons.

Sadly, many of us treat time like an unlimited resource. According to a 2018 Neilsen survey, "American adults spend over *eleven hours per day* listening to, watching, reading or generally interacting with media." Our time is valuable, at least to the advertisers paying to show us their products, but how much do *we* value it?

How we spend our time is important. When we waste our lives in front of a screen, we miss opportunities to glorify God, spread the Gospel, and pray. Our activities are self-serving rather than God-honoring.

Psalm 90 ends with an appeal for God to imbue our lives with significance. "May the favor of the Lord our God rest on us; establish the work of our hands for us—yes, establish the work of our hands" (Psalm 90:17 NIV).

Your days are numbered, and your time is valuable. How will you choose to spend it?

---

*Have you ever measured your average daily screen time? How could your time be put to better use?*

# BE THE MAN WHO IS A CLEAN VESSEL

*In a large house there are articles not only of gold and silver, but also of wood and clay; some are for special purposes and some for common use. Those who cleanse themselves from the latter will be instruments for special purposes, made holy, useful to the Master and prepared to do any good work.*
2 TIMOTHY 2:20–21 NIV

According to a 2020 report from the National Coffee Association, 62 percent of Americans drink coffee daily, and the number of people surveyed who reported drinking coffee within the past day has risen by 5 percent since 2015. Whether at home, in a restaurant, or at the office, there's one thing all coffee drinkers prefer: a clean cup.

We may differ over light roast or dark roast and whether coffee should be enjoyed black or with cream and sugar, but no one argues for drinking from a filthy mug. We don't stop there though: Most people have a favorite mug. According to researchers, nearly

60 percent of us have an "emotional attachment" to our favorite mug, and 38 percent would consider hiding it so others couldn't use it.

Now imagine the roof starts leaking over your desk. Ideally, you'd grab a bucket to catch the water, but your favorite coffee mug is already beside you. Or imagine needing a place to put a bunch of flowers. A vase would be your first choice, but what if the mug was closer? In either case, the next time you wanted coffee, you'd definitely make sure your mug was cleaned out before pouring in some java again.

In 2 Timothy, Paul compares us to household vessels. Some are made of gold and others from clay. But it doesn't matter what we're made of; if we are clean and willing, we'll be set aside and "made holy, useful to the Master and prepared to do any good work" (2 Timothy 2:21 NIV).

Want to be God's favorite mug? Start by asking Him to cleanse you. Then be willing to do whatever He asks.

---

*How are you like your favorite mug?*
*What might God need to cleanse in*
*you before you are willing to be used?*

# BE THE MAN WHO KNOWS HOW TO BE GENTLE

*Always be humble and gentle. Be patient with each other, making allowance for each other's faults because of your love.*
EPHESIANS 4:2 NLT

---

Relative to their size, jaguars have the strongest bite force—about 1,500 pounds per square inch (psi)—of any of the world's big cats. For comparison, humans bite with a force between 150–200 psi. Jaguars, unlike other big cats, which go for the throat, kill by crushing the skulls of their prey. Even so, jaguars also use their jaws to carefully carry their young.

As cubs, jaguars are born with their eyelids sealed shut, and they can't open them for about two weeks. They don't start learning to hunt or fend for themselves until they're about six months old. Until then, they are completely vulnerable and require their mother's constant attention.

Weakness is like a newborn jaguar cub, while gentleness is like a jaguar mother caring for that cub.

Mistaking one for the other could be fatal. Being gentle implies the restraining—not deficiency—of strength.

Likewise, humility is not the absence of greatness. It is the decision not to brag when the world thinks we could.

For the man of purpose, this behavior is the natural response to God's gentleness and humility toward us. Colossians 3:12 (NLT) says, "Since God chose you to be the holy people he loves, you must clothe yourselves with tenderhearted mercy, kindness, humility, gentleness, and patience."

If God has chosen you to be His child, you can choose to restrain your strength while dealing with others and remain silent when you feel like bragging. Only then will others see Him in you.

---

*Have you ever confused weakness with gentleness? How can you better restrain your strength so others can see God in you?*

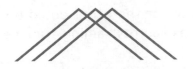

# BE THE MAN
# WHO STAYS COOL

*Have no fear of sudden disaster or of the ruin that overtakes the wicked, for the LORD will be at your side and will keep your foot from being snared.*
PROVERBS 3:25–26 NIV

Insurance salesmen love to pitch their products as peace of mind for people entering risky situations. Homes and vehicles, unexpected medical costs, and even the death of a loved one are all covered by various types of insurance. One London-based insurance firm has even sold more than thirty thousand alien abduction insurance policies throughout Europe, provided its policyholders have physical proof of their abduction.

Insurance companies thrive on the fear of uncontrollable circumstances. And while getting coverage for our belongings, health, and lives is important, we as God's children shouldn't fear the uncontrollable—since we know God controls everything.

Bad things happen, but we're not to react to them

as the world does. When earthquakes and wildfires strike, we can trust God. When people turn against us or enemies attack, we know God still fights for us and encourages us to react with love.

In Matthew 5:43–45 (NIV), Jesus says, "You have heard that it was said, 'Love your neighbor and hate your enemy.' But I tell you, love your enemies and pray for those who persecute you, that you may be children of your Father in heaven. He causes his sun to rise on the evil and the good, and sends rain on the righteous and the unrighteous."

Insurance doesn't hold a candle to the peace of mind God gives. Even if our physical belongings or bodies are destroyed, nothing can separate us from God's love (see Romans 8:38–39). He has not insured our lives against trouble. He has insured our souls against harm.

---

*Do you stay cool as the world around you burns? How can your eternal insurance help you navigate life when you experience trouble?*

# BE THE MAN WHO EMBRACES MANHOOD

*When I was a child, I spake as a child,*
*I understood as a child, I thought as a child:*
*but when I became a man, I put away childish things.*
1 CORINTHIANS 13:11 KJV

---

We'll never become men of purpose if we aren't willing to grow up. We must put away childish things, growing into our identities as men of God.

When other men chase after the things of this world, our priorities should be different. First Timothy 6:11 (NIV) says, "But you, man of God, flee from all this, and pursue righteousness, godliness, faith, love, endurance and gentleness."

Righteousness and godliness were made possible for us through Christ's sacrifice. Second Corinthians 5:21 (NIV) says, "God made him who had no sin to be sin for us, so that in him we might become the righteousness of God."

Our example will put us at odds with the world. Second Timothy 3:12–13 (NIV) says, "In fact, everyone who wants to live a godly life in Christ Jesus will be persecuted, while evildoers and impostors will go from bad to worse, deceiving and being deceived."

Even in persecution, though, we know we're on the right side.

As men, we must have faith stronger than doubt, love stronger than hate, endurance stronger than temptation, and gentleness stronger than anger. For all this, we need God's help.

Being a man doesn't mean going solo against the world. It means partnering with the One who has overcome the world, inviting Him into every area of our lives and freely admitting our need for His grace, mercy, strength, and peace.

When we embrace our purpose as men, we can share in Paul's joy and confidence "that he who began a good work in you will carry it on to completion until the day of Christ Jesus" (Philippians 1:6 NIV).

---

*Are you maturing in your faith? In what areas can you pray for God's assistance?*

# ANOTHER GREAT DEVOTIONAL FOR MEN

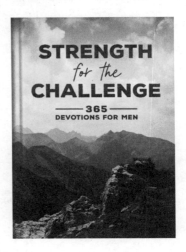

Guys, you know life can be tough. But never forget that God is strong. This daily devotional builds off the inspired truth of 2 Corinthians 12:10, "when I am weak, then I am strong." You'll be encouraged to seek your daily strength from the all-powerful God through Jesus Christ.

Hardcover / 978-1-64352-850-2 / $16.99